THE Hidden PARTNER

TRUE STORIES OF GOD AT WORK IN EVERYDAY LIFE

Rev. Percy V. Kooshian

THE HIDDEN PARTNER
TRUE STORIES OF GOD AT WORK IN EVERYDAY LIFE

iUniverse books may be ordered through booksellers or by contacting:

iUniverse
1663 Liberty Drive
Bloomington, IN 47403
www.iuniverse.com
1-800-Authors (1-800-288-4677)

ISBN: 978-1-5320-3291-2 (sc)
ISBN: 978-1-5320-3292-9 (e)

Library of Congress Control Number: 2017914049

Print information available on the last page.

iUniverse rev. date: 10/30/2017

TABLE OF CONTENTS

FOREWORD

The vicissitudes of life never seem to end – particularly when they are filled with the kind of adversity that weighs us down, causes us to whimper, and may even challenge our faith. In this book Rev. Kooshian offers a series of vignettes which recount memorable experiences, both as a military medic with his twin brother in Japan and as a pastor of two small Baptist churches. And incidentally, when we say "small church," we tend to mean "inadequate, limited, understaffed, deficient, needing to grow in numbers and grace." As you read one ordeal after another, you may be reminded of the opening words of a hymn,

> Earthly friends may prove untrue
> Doubts and fears assail;
> One still loves and cares for you,
> One who will not fail.

And that is the central message of the book: Jesus never fails.

Percy's struggles resonate with all of us. How do I find an evangelical church when I am overseas, tied to the military and don't know anyone? How do I cope with financial privation while serving as a leader in a church which is facing severe debt? How do I provide the next meal for my family or buy a car when I'm virtually penniless? How do I cope with a church split? How do I respond to a health crisis? What do I say to testy parishioners? Such perplexities may impel us to sing "Does Jesus Care?' or "Come Ye Disconsolate."

But Percy never lets us sink into the slough of despond, for each chapter concludes with the miracle of God's abundant supply. He suggests that we assimilate the principle that he learned years ago in his college hymn, "Great is Thy Faithfulness" - particularly "all I have needed thy hand hath provided." He reminds us that no one enjoys the trials of life, but everyone can benefit from them. How? They create patience, they develop sensitivity to others in need, they foment prayer, they foster praise, and they energize faith. In these stories we learn that God promises to supply "exceedingly abundantly above all that we ask or think."

Conflict, uncertainty, maltreatment, malevolence, turmoil – how should a Christian properly respond? In Max Lucado's brilliant treatise on Joseph, YOU'LL GET THROUGH THIS, one chapter exclaims, "Oh, So This Is Boot Camp!" Rehearsing the journey of Joseph, he asks, "For what purpose did God permit this?" "Is life a crash course in suffering?" Lucado concludes the chapter, "Don't see our struggle as an interruption to life, but a preparation for life…God is doing what is best for us, training us to live God's holy best." He follows with a chapter entitled "Is God Good When Life Isn't?" which asks, "Is God angry at me?" "Did the devil outwit him?" "Where is He in all of this?" Pastor Kooshian suggests in his narrative that we simply remember what the Bible teaches: God is good, He is love, He promises to supply all my need, and all things work together for good to them who love Him.

This is a book that will comfort the afflicted, encourage the forlorn, and strengthen the fainthearted. In essence, our pastor narrator is declaring, "As a young believer, a Bible student, and an active worker in God's vineyard, I experienced unusual and vexatious circumstances. But in all of this I realized that God was with me, and His grace was always sufficient. God is the potter; we are just the vessels being shaped. He is the shepherd; we are merely the sheep. God is the vine; we are just branches."

As a husband, father, pastor and 'just everyday Christian, Percy wants us to know that "nothing is impossible when you put your trust in God."

Dr. W. James DeSaegher
Point Loma Nazarene University
San Diego, California

PREFACE

Born into an immigrant family during the Great Depression, I learned at an early age that money was not plentiful. Frugality became an important value to our family. By prudent thriftiness, our family survived in those difficult depression years. Further, our parents trusted in God to meet their daily needs and taught their children to do the same.

At the age of 8 years old, I became a believer in Christ, much to the joy of my godly parents. At the age of 22, having graduated from Westmont College, I was inducted into military service. Returning from active duty, I was accepted by Fuller Theological Seminary as a ministerial student and spent four years preparing for ministry.

Armed with a seminary education and blessed with a beautiful young wife, I looked forward to serving the Lord. Possessing no savings, but having received a call to serve on staff at a church in La Mesa, California, we moved there, and took charge of the church's education ministry. Our three children were born during the first years of our ministry.

It was in 1970 that our lives took a sharp turn as we entered the pastorate in Cottage Grove, Oregon. The years of national recession in the 1970's, were felt severely in South Lane County. Jobs were not available as the wood industry collapsed. Because the church was failing financially, we suddenly found ourselves facing severe want and need.

However, we learned through experience that the provision of God was at once, creative, exciting and beyond our expectations. My wife, Carolyn, urged me to write about God's faithful provision both in my formative years and in our married life. As a family we all marveled at the Hand of God supplying our earthly needs through our Lord Jesus Christ.

The stories contained in this volume are true. We share them with you because we believe that if God provided for us in such wonderful ways during the lean times, He can do the same for you. Unseen, God is truly the Hidden Partner. It is my hope that you find encouragement from these stories of God's creative power.

Percy V. Kooshian
August 1, 2017

ACKNOWLEDGEMENTS

An author's name on the cover of a book may leave an impression of singular talent and effort. That is not so. Many people are involved to whom thanks are due.

Thanks to the good folks at iUniverse for their encouragement and assistance in guiding me through the process of putting together a volume worth reading.

Dr. W. James DeSaegher, a Westmont College friend and classmate, patiently corrected the text, gently reminding me that my grasp of English grammar could benefit from taking a few more college courses. His expertise and encouragement are greatly appreciated.

Thanks to the close filial partnership of my late twin brother, Roy, who shared the early blessings of God with me.

I am deeply indebted to my wife and our three children who witnessed the amazing evidence of God's loving interest and support over the passage of time.

Most of all, thanks be to God Who provided all of our needs.

INTRODUCTION

When God steps into the natural world and supersedes the laws of nature, that is a miracle. Most of us do not live on that level. But when God provides for our everyday needs and requirements for living, that can be identified as the exciting provision of the Hidden Partner.

"So don't worry at all about having enough food and clothing. Why be like the heathen? For they take pride in all these things and are deeply concerned about them. But your heavenly Father already knows perfectly well that you need them, and he will give them to you if you give him first place in your life and live as he wants you to." Matthew 6:31-33. (Living Bible)

1

Lesson in Physiology
June 1952

The popular young student approaching us looked shocked. Her eyes indicated that she was on the verge of tears as she exited the science classroom. John Muir Junior College in Pasadena, California combined the last two years of high school with the first two years of college in an academic experiment of the Pasadena school system. It was the end of our freshman college year, and my twin brother, Roy, and I were approaching the physiology classroom to pre-register in advance for the next school year, the same classroom Janet Larson had just left. Janet was the envy of many students. Highly gifted, attractive, athletic, and musically talented, she exhibited a sparkling personality. She also was at the top of her graduating class, winning the coveted honor of valedictorian.

As the valedictorian, she was justifiably proud of her heretofore perfect grades. But her perfect academic record had just been shattered by the B- grade she had received in the physiology class. Even though it did not affect her standing as the valedictorian that year, she was deeply upset that her perfect academic record had been erased by a single grade. The fact that she was still academically at the top of the student body and that her position as valedictorian was still secure did not seem to assuage her grief at the inexplicable grade she had just received.

While Roy and I did not know her well, she recognized us because we were identical twins. Perhaps it was also because of our practice of cheerfully greeting our fellow students whenever we passed them in the school halls between classes. As she greeted us through eyes glistening with tears, her expression crumbled, and she blurted out her anguish. "Are you planning to take this class?" she asked as we made for the door, registration forms in hand. "Yes," Roy replied. I nodded. "We have to take it as a requirement for graduation next year." Shaking her head as her curls swirled around her face, she warned, "Don't take this class. Dr. Swanson is so tough that he will not accept anything except absolutely perfect assignments!"

Indeed, Dr. Erik Swanson was reputed to be one of the most demanding teachers in the institution. "I can't believe that my perfect grade point average has been destroyed by one teacher," she lamented, tears beginning to course down her cheeks. Politely, Roy offered her his handkerchief, which she gratefully accepted. "You are the best student in this school," Roy emphatically declared. "What happened?" In a broken voice Janet replied, "That was the hardest class I ever took. I guess that physiology just isn't my subject." Dabbing at her eyes with the white hanky, she continued, "I can't believe it! I did my best. I would have had a perfect GPA." Patting her arm rather awkwardly, I offered the best support I could at that moment. "Well, you are still tops in our books!" Returning the handkerchief to Roy, she smiled "Thanks. I really appreciate that." She sniffed, regained her composure and continued down the hall.

Stunned by the encounter, Roy and I watched the most accomplished student in school shuffle down the hallway, burdened by her sorrow.

Glancing at each other, Roy and I realized that we still had to register for the same class that had proven to be such a difficult challenge for Janet Larson. As we looked at each other, our minds focused upon the same thought. *"If the valedictorian of the school could not maintain her "A" average in Dr. Swanson's class, what chance will we have to pass?"* The question hung between us, unspoken and unanswered. We were not accomplished students. We did not view ourselves as "gifted" because our grades were academically average. The encounter with Janet Larson now forcefully imprinted on our minds, we pushed through the doorway and entered the classroom.

As we entered the room crowded with an orderly arrangement of worktables upon which lay a variety of microscopes, alcohol lamps and exotic glassware, we spotted Dr. Swanson sitting at his desk surrounded by a group of students. He was dressed casually, a white, unbuttoned lab coat draped over his sport shirt and slacks. As we drew nearer, we could hear the indignant clamor for an explanation of the grades which each of the students had received.

Dr. Erik Swanson's casual attire failed to communicate a relaxed demeanor. The intensity of his stern expression communicated a hint of anger as he answered each student with an edge in his voice. To one determined objector he growled, "You didn't turn in your assignments on time." To another crestfallen coed, he replied in a gentler tone, "Your experiments were sloppy." To the demand of an indignant football team member's hoarse query, "How come I got a "D"? he answered, "With your test grades, you were lucky to pass this course." He continued to shake his head in wonderment and disbelief at the students who were demanding an explanation for the low grades that reflected their poor performances in his class.

With some degree of trepidation, Roy and I approached the professor whose reputation for demanding excellence was well known throughout the student body. As we gingerly edged our way through the group with our class registration forms firmly gripped in our hands, we broke through the small crowd of students and came suddenly face to face with the tense visage of this feared professor. Looking at us with our extended registration forms, he scowled. "Why do you boys want to take this class?" Taken aback by his aggressive question, I hesitated. "Uh," Roy stammered, "we have to take this class as a requirement for graduation." "Well, good luck," snarled Dr. Swanson as he hastily scribbled his initials on each of our class applications. Then, with a dismissive gesture, he turned away to yet another anguished student. As the clamor increased, Roy and I made a hasty exit from the classroom, wondering vocally to each other what the next school year would hold for us.

Summer vacation was filled with work, church activities and recreational opportunities. But even through the leisurely pace of summer, a vague nagging anxiety began to lodge itself in our minds as we fearfully anticipated the new school year with Dr. Swanson's class in physiology. *Would we fail miserably in class as we feared?* Although Roy and I did not speak of it, our trepidation rose as the summer vacation came to an end. All too soon the fall semester of school arrived.

Even with the novelty of new classes, which were filled with friends both old and new, we looked ahead with apprehension to the last class of the day, Physiology 101. True to our fears, the initial class session was overwhelming as a thick syllabus was handed to each student. Opening the syllabus, I was overwhelmed by a visual assault of complex diagrams, detailed anatomical drawing and unfamiliar scientific terms. Suddenly I was aware of Dr. Swanson's presence beside my seat as he handed me the yearly assignment sheet. As I perused the pages of our reading assignments, lab instructions, expected reports and the test schedule, Dr. Swanson's voice emphasized his high standards for the class. "I expect all of you to do your best in this class. I will not tolerate shoddy work! If you are lazy and do mediocre work, I will know it. And if you simply coast along in class, you will not pass!" We had no doubt that he meant what he said. Dr. Swanson expected exceptional diligence in our lab work, exacting detail in our experiments and meticulous accuracy in our reports. Hanging from a frame near the professor's desk were the bones of a full-sized human skeleton. The toothy skull which faced the classroom seemed to grin in silent agreement with the professor.

As time went by, and as the class work progressed, our assignments grew increasingly difficult. Roy and I began to pray each night before opening the physiology textbook to complete our homework, which became a regular practice during the year. We prayed that we would understand the material, complete the experiments on time, and be prompt in turning in the assigned homework. Our prayers were simple and direct. "Dear God, please help us to understand the syllabus. And help us to do the best we can in our assignments and experiments." While we were not aware at the time of Proverbs 16:3, we began to become more enthusiastic about the class. As we prayed over our homework, we found that our grades were beginning to improve immeasurably.

Toward the end of the semester as finals week approached, Dr. Swanson made an unusual announcement. "Final exams are in two weeks. Some of you really need to study because you are behind. All of you will benefit if you begin this evening to prepare for the final exams. That is, all of you except the Kooshian twins and Nancy Harper. They have such superior grades that they will be exempt from the final exams. They are the top three students in the class." Then, addressing us, he added, "Congratulations to you three. You have been a credit to this class by your superior work. Your 'A' grades are assured without your having to take the final exam."

Roy and I were amazed! *How could we excel in a class which the valedictorian of last year had found to be exceedingly difficult? It could only be that God had answered our prayers and honored us for putting Him first in our physiology class.* Only later did the words of Proverbs 16:3 (NASB) come to our attention. "Commit your works to the LORD And your plans will be established." We learned a valuable lesson that year.

2

Preposterous Pay Scale
July 1953

Summer jobs were scarce in 1953. Unaware of the condition of the national economy, Roy and I were naively ignorant of the difficulty of obtaining jobs at that time. A downturn in the economy beginning in April of that year lasted for 12 months. This recession, which was described as "mild and brief" by a staff member of the national Bureau of the Budget, nevertheless negatively affected the job market.

My twin brother and I had just graduated from John Muir Junior College. The graduation from 14th grade carried with it an Associate in Arts degree, the first step in our post-high school ambitions. But a new challenge faced us. We had been accepted by a prestigious Christian liberal arts institution of higher learning and were looking forward to attending Westmont College in the fall. However, the cost per school year for this elite private college was formidable. Even before college education costs rose to present levels, the sum of $1,500 a year (in 1953) was an intimidating financial challenge, especially for two students from a single family with a modest income.

Consequently, Roy and I were desperate for summer jobs which would help us to pay for our initial semester at Westmont. So, when "Uncle" Luther Eskijian, who owned the Eskijian Construction Company, offered us employment, we eagerly accepted. "Uncle" Luther was a gifted architect and developer. His building designs and construction accomplishments included large industrial buildings as well as residential land developments in many cities and communities spread across Southern California. As a leader and benefactor of the Armenian community he was well-known and wielded significance influence among Armenians. Since he was a student of our father back in Turkey during the genocide of the Moslem Turks against the Christian Armenians, he felt close to our family. So, when we applied to him for a job on one of his construction crews, he readily accepted us. Because he understood that Roy and I had led a comparatively sheltered life and needed to be exposed to the realities of the working world, he instructed his foreman, "Don't coddle these boys. They need to learn what the real world is about. Give them tasks to do, starting at the bottom of the ladder, but don't tell them how to do them. Simply, let them figure it out for themselves."

Since Roy and I were classified as "unskilled labor," we soon found ourselves as common laborers with shovels in our hands. Our first work assignment was a four-foot deep, three-foot wide, forty-foot long trench, dug through rocky soil, presenting a fair challenge to two inexperienced college boys. The trench was in preparation for a solid concrete foundation to support a heavy, three-story cement block wall which constituted one side of the educational unit of the Pasadena Jewish Community Center. After laying out the location and parameters of the trench with string and wooden stakes, we began at one end with our first shovel of dirt.

Returning home after the first day, both Roy and I discovered sore muscles which we either did not know existed or had long forgotten from our studies in physiology. My shoulders and upper arms were stiff with pain from the constant effort of the repetitive motions of digging. Even my wrists, hands and legs ached from the intense effort of digging in rocky soil. Roy felt the same. I asked, "Roy, are you as stiff and sore as I am?" He grimaced, tersely answered, "More." And this was only after the first day! Having barely begun, Roy and I still had the entire

40-foot trench to complete. We both slept soundly that night – the sleep of honest exhaustion.

As day followed day with little variety in our activity, several conclusions began to form in my mind all based upon the presupposition that ditch-digging was a lowly profession. With nothing more than the sinking of a shovel into the soil and then throwing the shovelful of dirt out over the lip of the trench, I began to observe some differences between ourselves and the rest of the construction crew.

First, I discovered that ditch-digging was regarded as a lowly profession because the pay of ditch diggers was at the bottom of the construction wage scale. As Roy and I removed the rocky, clayish soil shovelful-by-shovelful, it dawned upon me that ours was not rated highly among the construction arts.

At noon, when the construction crew sat together in the shade for a lunch break, I could feel the social distance as the camaraderie shared by the other members of the construction crew did not include my brother and me. It was not because we were new to the crew, but was because we were different. While they worked together, Roy and I were isolated on an undeveloped part of the building site, preparing for a future foundation. We were acutely aware that the construction crew regarded us as a couple of "college boys" who were inexperienced and ignorant regarding the necessary skills for the building trade. Our references to "Uncle Luther" served to isolate us further from the camaraderie of these men who had worked together for many years on various building projects and who regarded Luther Eskijian as their employer.

A second observation regarding the construction crew's reserve toward us seemed to be directly related to our filthy appearance. Standing in the excavation of the trench, we were vulnerable to the dust and dirt which accumulated on our clothes and bodies as the day's labor wore on. By the end of the work day, Roy and I were easily the filthiest workers on the job. (At home when we showered, the water ran brown into the drain.)

Further, the fact that we were "college boys" among workers who regarded education with suspicion placed another barrier between us. Since they regarded "experience" to be of a higher practical value than "book learning," they were not shy about sharing their feelings with us.

However, the most significant reason for the distance between the others in the construction crew and the two "ditch-diggers" on the crew was the stigma attached to the phrase "common laborer." It was a phrase which represented the lowest level of the working force, as in "He's nothing but a common laborer!" Any task which the carpenters identified as below their professional expertise they dismissed with a vulgar profanity, followed by "let the laborers do it," calling upon us to perform any unwanted chore that they deemed beneath their journeyman status.

Despite the differences which clearly separated us from the rest of the construction crew, Roy and I were glad to be employed. While we were generally politely accepted, we felt the separation between us and those involved in the professional skilled trades - plumbers, electricians, truckers, heavy equipment operators, pavers, roofers, and cabinet makers. These all made their appearance at some time or other on the job site. And each time some new tradesman showed up on the scene, we became subtly aware that we were different by comparison.

As the summer days progressed, the temperature rose. During the hot weather, Roy and I would arise at 5:00 a.m. and reach the job site by 6:00 a.m. so that we could shovel dirt in the cool of the morning. Even with the early start, we were still at work when the day began to heat up, so the last few hours of our shift were often spent in blistering heat. As soon as Uncle Luther took notice of the heat, he began to assign us other jobs. In the early morning hours, we would continue with shovel and spade to dig the foundational trench. But in the heat of the day, we would be assigned tasks inside the partially completed building, where a roof and walls offered shade.

It took us a couple of weeks to complete the trench. As we progressed, we began to take pride in our work when we saw the straight, precise dimensions of our completed project. It never occurred to us at that time that the job could have been completed in a single day using trenching equipment. Apparently, Uncle Luther was extending himself to give us jobs at a time when jobs were scarce.

As the summer wore on, a subtle change began to take place. Because Roy and I tried to be unfailingly courteous and cooperative, we began to feel the hesitant acceptance of the members of the construction crew. With the foundational trench completed in a neat, strait line, we were assigned to tasks much closer to the other workers. Before long we became regarded as part of the crew.

Our next assignments included driving the dump trucks to the landfill, assisting carpenters as they directed us, returning equipment to the tool rental agencies, and cement work. When it became time to raise the huge twelve-inch-thick beams, twenty-five-feet long, into an upright position as supports for the steel beams that supported the second story of the building, we became an integral part of the building team. Soon we were being included in more specialized tasks that presented themselves in the normal course of construction.

One memorable week, Uncle Luther reassigned us to a project in the southern Mojave Desert. The development was just outside of Desert Hot Springs, a small, rather primitive community at that time. Our task was to lay water pipeline for a proposed residential development. While Uncle Luther drove a truck slowly down the graded dirt road, Roy and I would run behind the truck and remove a length of 16-foot pipe to place beside the road. It was hot, strenuous work. In the evenings, Uncle Luther would take us to dinner at a local resort followed by a refreshing time in the cool, clear waters of the resort pool. He seemed to take delight in treating us to some relaxation following a hot day of work. When he worked, he did so with intensity. When he relaxed, he enjoyed himself to the fullest. When the pipeline was in place, we returned to Pasadena and rejoined the construction crew.

And so the summer passed day-by-day while Roy and I learned more and more about the various aspects of the construction trade. There was no doubt that we were now accepted by the members of the crew. Their reserve gone, they accepted us even to the degree of respecting our moments of saying silent grace in thanksgiving for our food.

One day late in the summer, while picking up debris from inside the nearly-completed building, I heard a voice call, "Hey, college boy!" It was the voice of a young man about my age, engaged in applying mud and tape to the bare sheetrock on the inner walls of the huge structure. He was not a member of the construction crew but an employee of a sub-contractor. After discovering that I was a college student, working as a laborer, he jeered, "How much do you make?" I answered him with an amount per hour that was the average pay for common labor. He bragged, "I make twenty-one dollars an hour. And I'm only a high school graduate." Smiling with scorn, he concluded, "A lot of good a college education does! Why don't you guys get a real job like mine instead of going off to some college and reading books?" He disagreed when I replied that there were other worthy goals in life besides devoting myself to making a lot of money.

As fall approached, our summer jobs ended. One day, as we were packing in preparation for college, Uncle Luther stopped by our house. "I have something for you boys," he said, handing us each a plain envelope, inside each of which was a very generous check. Uncle Luther dismissed our wide-eyed thanks. "It is a bonus for your summer work. You boys did good work on the crew." Smiling, he concluded as he left, "I want to make sure that you boys get a good education." We were stunned by his big-heartedness.

I was very curious to see how much this additional undeserved bonus, tendered through the kindness and magnanimity of Uncle Luther, would have boosted my hourly wage for my summer work. Adding the bonus check to the sum of my summer wages and dividing that by the total hours worked, the resulting average hourly wage was far higher than that of the braggart who had derided a college education.

Roy and I completed that college year without debt, thanks to Uncle Luther. We had enough for our tuition. Our parents had also helped significantly by making all our clothes since they both excelled in tailoring skills.

Years later, after Uncle Luther had passed away, I recounted his generosity to his gracious wife and widow, Auntie Anne Eskijian. She smiled at my story and then turned serious. "He was always doing things like that. He especially loved you boys and was very proud of you."

Once again, God had used an unexpected source to meet our financial needs. Surely the promises of God prove to be sure and certain.

3

Cause and Effect
December 1954

It seemed hopeless. As college seniors, my twin brother and I were in desperate need of money. After having completed two years of junior college, we had felt led of the Lord to attend Westmont College, a prestigious Christian liberal arts institution in Santa Barbara, California, just over a hundred miles from home. The $1,500 yearly tuition per student was an enormous amount in 1955, our graduation year. Now we faced the last semester of our senior year of college and needed to earn enough to pay off our debts before graduation. It was the pre-Christmas season, and we were on Christmas break.

The morning after we arrived home, we rushed downtown to the main post office. Hurrying up the wide stone steps through the multi-arched doors into the cavernous lobby, we did not take time to notice the classical architecture of the building with its red tile roof and huge stone construction. Built in 1913 in the Italian renaissance style, it was one of the anchoring buildings of the "Old Pasadena" complex which included the city hall, the public library and the civic auditorium. Always crowded with postal patrons, the large interior with its high ceiling managed to muffle the sounds of shuffling feet, business transactions, and postal machines.

We stood in line before one of the post office service windows, anxiety written on our faces. "Do you think that we have a chance for a job?" I directed the question to Roy as the line moved forward. "I don't know," he replied. "It's pretty late in the pre-Christmas season. I would guess that all the jobs are pretty well filled by now.' I nodded my head in silent agreement. "At least we can try," I encouraged.

Before long it was our turn to stand facing the clerk behind the window. Leaning forward to speak distinctly thorough the wrought iron barrier, I asked in a respectful tone, "Sir, are there any openings for employment as Christmas mail carriers?" The clerk stamped a large envelope before him, and glancing up, shook his head. "No, I think that all positions for Christmas mail carriers were filled last week." As he reached for another envelope, I asked again, "Is there anyone we can see who can help us?" His expression softened as he observed the discouragement written on our faces. "You can check in with the Christmas labor supervisor for any possible openings in the event of some last-minute cancellation. He might be able to help you." Then he added, "You can find him in the back. Just go through that door," gesturing toward a door leading into the interior of the building.

With heavy hearts, we entered the interior of the post office. We knew that without the generous wages that Christmas mail delivery offered, we would be hard-pressed to pay our college debts before graduation. We wound our way through the maze of carts overflowing with packages, bulging sacks of mail, and sorting desks whose numbered cubbyholes were jammed with undelivered envelopes. None of the uniformed postal employees looked up from their engrossing tasks to stop or question us. Leaving the scurrying postal employees behind, we passed into a dimly lit portion of the building and came upon a desk set far against the back wall.

There, in the relative quietness and obscurity of an isolated area, an obviously weary man in a green visor sat amidst an overwhelming pile of papers and forms scattered across the surface of his desk. His desk lamp provided a pool of light in an otherwise darkened part of the building. His attention was fixed on an open file folder which had the word

"APPLICATIONS" printed on its front in large, bold block letters. If it was possible for our hopes to sink any further, they did, for we noted that the file folder could barely contain the stack of completed applications for the relatively few openings that were available for auxiliary mail delivery positions during the current Christmas season.

We waited patiently as he perused the form in his hands. As he set down the form and reached for another, Roy politely asked, "Are there any more positions open for Christmas postal employment?" Without looking up, he shook his head, confirming our worst fears, "No. They are all taken."

Thanking him, we began to turn away when he glanced up and asked, "Say, don't I know you boys?" We did not recognize him. To our reply, "We don't think so," he countered with dawning recognition, "Yes, I know you. Didn't you boys work at the Gertmenian's grocery store a few years back?"

It was true. We had worked for our "Uncle" Manual Gertmenian in his grocery store during our high school years. During that time, people from all economic levels came in to shop for the special items that lured customers into the market. Those from the lowest economic brackets, of course were often treated more perfunctorily than others reflecting higher social levels. But it was not a purposeful prejudice. Several nationalities made up the shopping public which crowded the grocery aisles and lanes between the fruit and vegetable bins. Some did not speak English well. Others were poor and had difficulty paying for the most basic of supplies. While "Uncle" Manual was generous to a fault, a few of his employees expressed their exasperation and impatience with those for whom the English language posed a challenge and for those whose dress and style betrayed their lower socioeconomic level. Those for whom bargaining was a way of life in their old culture could not understand the blunt hostility of store employees, who were unaccustomed to such a foreign cultural practice. One man, who had lost an arm at the shoulder, was disrespectfully addressed as "Bandit," reminiscent of the single-lever gambling devices nicknamed "one arm bandits." If he felt any resentment, he did not show it. However, as Roy and I assisted him with his bags and were careful to address him as "sir," he seemed to appreciate our respect.

Roy and I had been brought up to treat everyone with respect, a value ingrained in us by our Christian parents. We were convinced that it represented not only our Christian duty but presented a good reflection upon our Lord. Consequently, we went out of our way to offer our assistance to those who had questions or who encountered difficulties in their shopping experience. We did it as a matter of expected Christian character.

The Christmas mail supervisor warmed up. "Yes, I remember you boys. You are the twins who were always nice to me even though some of the other employees there were rude and impatient. Yes," he remembered, "you always treated me with respect and carried out my packages, refusing any tips." His smile deepened with remembered recognition. "Yes," he repeated, "I remember you."

A faint memory grew in my consciousness. Our past employment at Gertmenian's Market flashed into my mind as I remembered a quiet man who spoke little and who was almost passive when paying for his groceries at the checkout stand. The memory of the impatience of some of the store clerks at the cash register during rush hours as this customer fumbled awkwardly with the coins in his palm suddenly came into sharp focus. It seemed almost remarkable that I remembered anything about past experiences at the grocery store during the crush of customers at the busiest time of the day. Yet here was one of those customers now occupying a position of influence and authority in the dim quietness at the rear of the main post office. Reserved as he was, we recognized that he wielded authority in his position as a postal supervisor. The current possibility of our employment throughout the Christmas season lay directly in his hands.

Shuffling through a stack of papers, he found what he was looking for and withdrew a job assignment list. Studying it, he asked, "Now, where would you boys like to work? You can have your choice of any substation in the city." We protested, "But you said that all the positions were filled." He smiled, "I'm the supervisor.' Pausing, he continued, "Now, where would you like to work?" His smile broadened as he assigned us to the most coveted positions in the city in a postal substation very near to our home. Dismissing our sudden flow of gratitude, he concluded, "Glad to be of help. Merry Christmas."

Later that evening over the dinner table, we joyfully recounted our unusual experience at the post office while our godly parents listened in amazement, praising God for His provision. It was then that Mother reminded us of the inexorable truth of one of her favorite verses in the Bible, (Ecclesiastes 11:1) "Cast thy bread upon the waters: for thou shalt find it after many days."

Every cause has its effect. In this case, an investment in courtesy resulted in the return of kindness and the unexpected provision of a Christmas job.

4

Before You Ask
June 1955

The final three weeks of our senior year at Westmont College were just ahead. Even after working summer jobs, carrying mail during Christmas breaks, and participating in the work/study programs at the college, my brother, Roy, and I still needed $300 each to completely pay for our college tuition. As twins, and as roommates, we shared the same mail box in the college post office.

On the day before finals week commenced, we discovered that a notice from the finance department of the college had arrived, informing us that we would be ineligible to receive our diplomas unless all college debts were paid prior to graduation. The payment due-date was only two weeks off. Our shock at receiving the notice simply reflected our ignorance. In retrospect, it seemed perfectly logical. Debts should be paid prior to graduation. Otherwise, what leverage did the college possess to enforce payments of student debts?

Our first glimpse of Westmont College had been at a visitation day almost three years before. On that occasion in 1952, as Roy and I faced our final year of junior college and were looking forward to finishing our education at a four-year institution, our youth pastor had taken several of the junior college students from our church to visit Westmont College. The campus was like no other college campus we had ever seen. Located in the foothills of Santa Barbara, California, it was situated on three lavish estates in the plush Montecito area where the world-famous, the wealthy and the powerful lived in extravagance out of public scrutiny. High walls and lush tropical growth shielded lavish, multi-acre properties with their magnificent residences from the scrutiny of inquisitive eyes. Three of those estates now constituted Westmont College.

The last event of our visit at the Westmont College Visitation Day was a session with the current president of the student body. Ed Hayes was handsome, with a disarmingly friendly demeanor. He related that, four years earlier, he had felt the Lord leading him to Westmont even though he had no financial prospect of attending such a prestigious private college. But in obedience to the Lord, he had applied and been accepted for his freshman year at the college. And now, four years later, he was graduating, with all his college debts paid thanks to the Lord's provision. Concluding his welcoming speech, he reached into his pocket and smiled, "And I even have thirty-seven cents left over." Laughter greeted his humorous demonstration of divine provision. However, Roy and I were fascinated by Ed's story. Nothing like that had ever happened to us.

"Is that really true?" I directed the question to Ed Hayes following the conclusion of the session, as we stood with others in a small circle around this personable and openly friendly young man. Ed must have read the expression of incredulity on my face as he answered, "Yes, it is," adding, "If the Lord is leading you to attend Westmont, He will provide for your expenses. God did it for me. He can do the same for you. Just follow His will. You will be surprised at what He will do for you." It was a challenge to put into practice what we mentally believed about God. With that encouragement, Roy and I decided to follow what we had accepted as the Lord's leading for our lives. and enrolled at Westmont for the fall term.

Now, close to graduation, we faced the end of our educational experience at Westmont which was only three weeks away. The problem facing us was that the books would be closed on the school financial year only two weeks away. And we were $600 short! It was time to face reality. Either what Ed Hayes had told us two years ago at the Westmont College Visitation Day was simply religious rhetoric, or it was time for Roy and me to put our profession of faith into practice.

We were familiar with the impressive Bible story of the Judean King, Hezekiah (as recorded in II Kings 19), who spread a threatening letter from the enemy Assyrian general, Rabshakeh, before the Lord in the Temple in Jerusalem as he prayed for deliverance from the frightening military superiority of the Assyrian army. In that desperate circumstance, God sent angelic help to Hezekiah. In one night, an angel of the Lord defeated the entire Assyrian army.

Without any pretence on our part, we thought that Hezekiah's example was the one to follow in our dire financial circumstance. Overwhelmed by the urgency of the situation we went to our room and, clearing books and homework from one of the two student desks in our room, laid the notice on the desktop. In desperation, we each prayed in our own words the following sentiment: "Dear Lord, please read this! We cannot graduate without paying the $600 we owe together within these two weeks before graduation. We believe that You called us to this school. Now we are depending on You to help us. We have tried everything to earn money, but it just isn't enough. We don't know anything else to do. Please help us." Yet I confess that despite our pleas to Almighty God, I could feel a nagging spirit of doubt. As far as either Roy or I knew, no one (other than God) knew of our plight except our parents and ourselves.

Our parents had supported us in every way they could. As professional tailors, they had made all our clothes for college, so we were well dressed. On our monthly trips home, they loaded us with Mom's great cooking to make sure we ate well. And they prayed daily for us. They even met many of our incidental expenses to ease our life at college.

In that pre-digital age, mail from home took a minimum of three days to reach us. Yet, on the second day after our desperate prayer session, an envelope appeared in our school mailbox. It was a check from our home church with a brief unsigned note: "This gift comes from an anonymous source, who thought that you might need some money just about now." The check was for $600, exactly enough to meet our school bills!

Not until much later did I happen upon this truth from Isaiah 65:23, "And it shall come to pass, that before they call, I will answer; and while they are yet speaking, I will hear."

Now, firmly lodged in my memory, that truth helps to remind me of God's power and enables me to understand the perplexing timing of God's provision for our college needs even before we prayed. Subject to the passage of time, we can grow anxious as deadlines approach. But our eternal God is not subject to time. He can reach down into our temporal existence and provide divine assistance at any given moment.

5

On the Marunouchi Line
October 1956

Seven months after our graduation from Westmont College, Roy and I found ourselves drafted into the United States Army. Six months of medical school followed our completion of three months of basic training. Upon completion, our military assignment took us to the Orient. We were dispatched to work in what was then the largest military hospital in the Far East, Tokyo United States Army Hospital (TUSAH), just blocks from the Sumida River, the main watercourse that emptied into Tokyo Bay. A scant half mile from the heart of downtown Tokyo, TUSAH stood in an old geisha district with its rickshaws, pedicabs (bicycle-powered carriages), and osoba (noodle soup) carts. Small shops purveying tea, sushi, fireworks, lacquerware, kokeshi dolls, herbs, spices and other distinctly Japanese goods lined the small streets and alleyways that formed the tangle of thoroughfares in the environs surrounding the hospital. Cars, taxis, rickshaws and the ever-present pedicabs all competed for space in the narrow streets surrounding the hospital grounds.

While the work at the hospital was challenging, the standard of living at Camp Burness (our living quarters) was much more desirable than the assignment of those in the cold, damp foxholes on the Demilitarized Zone (DMZ) in Korea. As far as Military Occupational Service (MOS) was concerned, ours was as desirable as any in the armed services. We were fortunate that in a large "station hospital" such as TUSAH, we received hot meals, clean beds and comparatively comfortable living quarters. The level of professionalism in our specialty as medical technicians (later as surgical technicians) allowed us a degree of respect not usually accorded to non-commissioned personnel in other fields of military endeavor. Usually those with whom we came into contact needed our help. Those who had suffered accidents, disease, or gunshot wounds from Korea joined the usual clientele of army dependents (wives and children) who needed medical and surgical attention. The medical and surgical staff of the hospital enjoyed the mystique and prestige usually granted to those in the medical field. To the average patient, the title "surgical technician" hinted that we possessed medical knowledge not known by others in the military. In part that was true, but only because we worked with doctors on a surgical team, the mysteries of which were generally unknown to the average soldier.

Yet, with all the advantages of being where we were in a relatively peaceful country, far from the hot spots of the world, and looked upon with some sense of respect, Roy and I still felt lonely.

We were apparently the only two men who professed to be believers in a camp of several hundred whose lifestyles reflected no moral or spiritual compass. But despite the awesome responsibility weighing upon those involved in critical medical care, it seemed to Roy and me that most of our new acquaintances in the detachment at Camp Burness were either alcoholic, immoral or lawless. We were often invited by acquaintances to join them in the alcoholic bouts at local bars or to participate in their debauchery as they visited the variety of houses of prostitution that were readily accessible nearby. It was even hinted to us by some of the more lawless element that with our access to surgical supplies, we could profit from the theft and resale of expensive surgical equipment (or even, with our supposed surgical expertise, organize an underground abortion clinic). After a more careful observation of the men in our living quarters at Camp Burness, it became clear that any camaraderie with our fellow soldiers would depend upon our sharing a common interest in the drinking, womanizing, gambling, and petty lawlessness in which they were engaged, none of which interested us in the least. In the final analysis, we either continued in constant social and spiritual isolation or engaged in the activities of our fellow soldiers. Any attempts to share our faith with them were squelched almost immediately.

Some of the men escaped the drudgery and boredom of camp life by living with Japanese women off-base without the benefit of marriage. They would spend all their free time away from Camp Burness in the various neighborhoods and precincts scattered around Tokyo. It was a sad but common experience to see crying women holding small babies, inquiring after a soldier who had rotated home, abandoning the sham family he had created while stationed in Tokyo at the hospital.

It was easy to sympathize with the unfortunate women who had hoped for emotional and economic security while engaging in extra-marital relationships. Many of the men who had set up these sham homes were already married and simply had ignored the responsibility of informing the unfortunate women of that fact. Because of this kind of atmosphere, Camp Burness was not a place where we wanted to spend much time. The non-commissioned officers club across the parade ground from our wing of the barracks building was nothing more than a bar with a dance floor and a small area of tables, where couples could order from the limited snack and dinner menu to complement their drinks.

Roy and I thought that the hospital chapel services, which were held on Sundays, might be the answer to our need for Christian Fellowship, but the chaplain's sermon delivery was rather bland, replete with alarming indications of theological liberalism. He did not preach the Gospel as we understood it but rather delivered messages based on a vague sense of morality. Current events served as the source of many sermonic inspirations. He was frank about his theological liberalism, which denied the essentials of the Christian faith. He did not believe the Bible to be the inspired Word of God and thereby the sole rule for faith and practice, so it was not surprising that he was skeptical about the virgin birth of Christ and the truthfulness of the miracles in our Lord's ministry.

The other attendees at Sunday services were mainly patients of the hospital who would soon be returning to their units scattered across the duty stations of the Pacific Rim. After a few visits to the hospital chapel services, Roy and I simply stopped attending, for there was no sense of "Church," the cohesiveness of a spiritual family with the fellowship network that characterized the local congregations to which we were accustomed back in the United States.

But now we were growing increasingly desperate for Christian fellowship. None of our acquaintances among the hospital personnel knew of an English language church gathering other than services at various base chapels scattered at military bases such as Camp Drake, Tachikawa, or Washington Heights, far too distant across the vast expanse of Tokyo for us to visit. Even though we longed for Christian fellowship, weeks passed by as we sought to break out of the parameters of our isolation. As our loneliness deepened, Roy and I began to earnestly pray that God would somehow release us from the social and spiritual barriers surrounding us. We wanted to become part of a Christian fellowship where we could enjoy the comfort of mutual faith with fellow believers.

After many weeks had passed, Roy and I became excited to hear of a musical concert some distance away in a community on the outskirts of Tokyo, so we decided to take advantage of the cultural opportunity. Since the subway system in Tokyo was pervasive throughout the city and adjoining environs, operating on a strict schedule which was famous for its punctuality, it was our most convenient mode of travel. Sometimes subways, at other times elevateds, these commuter trains sped their human cargo to the far-flung towns and villages that surrounded the crowded city.

Tokyo Central Station was the hub of a complexity of train lines. The major train lines originating at Tokyo Central Station led out in various directions as serpentine spokes of a large transportation wheel, the rim of which was the Oedo Line, which roughly described an oval around the city. It was possible to ride endlessly around the city on the Oedo Line with a single ticket. Not so with the "spokes" of the railroad "wheel." The serpentine tracks (stretching from north to south, winding their way from east to west, and orientations in between) inevitably had to intersect the Oedo Line as they proceeded even further into the surrounding communities, towns and villages. Those commuter trains had engines on both ends of the passenger cars facing in opposite directions. When a train would reach the end of its line, the engineer would simply shut down the engine, place it into a neutral gear, walk through the cars to the other end of the train and start the engine that pointed in the opposite direction. Several lines operated in this back and forth mode many times a day. Of course, wherever train lines crossed each other, there was a station which allowed travelers to transfer from one train line to another.

We boarded an older commuter on the Marunouchi Line (one of the serpentine lines from Tokyo Station) and rode a winding path through neighboring communities which made up the metropolitan area of the largest city in the world. Crossing the Oedo line, the tracks soon led the commuter train out into the beautiful Japanese countryside. The darkening evening sky was reflected in the large flooded rice paddies which bordered the tracks. Intermittent stops at village stations gradually emptied the train cars of late travelers from the great city. Finally, Roy and I were all alone in our train car. As we pulled out of each station back into the fading twilight, distant terraced hillsides with their narrow rice paddies testified to the industry of the Japanese farmer. In a small country where arable land was precious, every possible piece of ground had to be dedicated to food production.

It was dark by the time we arrived at our destination. The venue for the event was a community hall. The concert was a beautiful and inspirational event, but the people were all strangers, so we did not feel that we could approach any of them with our search for Christian fellowship.

When Roy and I stepped aboard the commuter heading back to Tokyo Central Station, we found the train cars almost empty due to the late hour of the evening. As we sat on the bench seats facing the similar seats on the other side of the car, we spotted an attractive teen-age girl sitting beside her date, a handsome young airman in uniform. Their friendly conversation with each other was fun-filled and wholesome. I asked Roy in a low whisper, "Do you think that the couple sitting across from us are Christians?" Roy replied, "They sure act like it." Whispering between ourselves, we determined to approach them. Perhaps they knew of a church or Christian group that we might visit.

I crossed over to the couple and asked the girl, "Are you by any chance a Christian?" Roy had approached the airman and had asked him the same question. Startled by our blunt query, they nodded, "Yes." At their affirmative response, an excitement seized me. *"At last,"* I thought, *"God has provided a link to the Christian community!"* As the train sped along in the darkness from station to station, our conversation warmed. The young man and his date informed us about the Tokyo Evangelical Church that met in the Korean YMCA just a couple of blocks from Korakuen Station in Tokyo. The girl was the daughter of Reformed Presbyterian missionaries who had spent many years in church planting and Christian Education in Japan. The young airman with whom Roy spoke was stationed at Tachikawa Airbase on the west side of Tokyo. We spent the rest of their journey in excited conversation, getting to know them. As they left the train at their destination, we promised to see each other at church the next Sunday.

Boarding the train early the next Sunday, we rode the Marunouchi Line from Tokyo station, past Ochonomizu (Tea Water), on to Korakuen (Garden of Power) Station in Bunkyo (heart), a neighborhood in the great city. Emerging from the station on the bright Sunday morning, we were immediately aware of the huge Korakuen Stadium, a venue for soccer, baseball and large musical concerts by world-famous artists.

Radiating from the oval of the stadium like rays of the sun were small streets directing us away from the massive sports arena. Finding the street as we were instructed, we walked the two blocks to the building with a sign in English, Korean and Japanese, "Korean Y.M.C.A." As we entered, we were greeted warmly. Inside the large room were missionaries, servicemen, State Department families and nationals from a variety of Pacific Rim nations. This was the Tokyo International Evangelical Church.

We found two seats halfway toward the front and sat quietly, waiting for the service to begin. At some silent signal from the platform, the congregation arose and began to recite Psalm 133 in unison from memory.

"Behold, how good and how pleasant it is for brethren to dwell together in unity! It is like the precious ointment upon the head that ran down upon the beard, even Aaron's beard: that went down to the skirts of his garments; As the dew of Hermon, and as the dew that descended upon the mountains of Zion: for there the LORD commanded the blessing, even life for evermore."

That experience in church was the beginning of many new friendships among missionaries of several different denominations. It was also the start of warm fellowship with servicemen and women from the Army, Navy and Air Force. Further, our influence seemed to grow. Soon, the word was spread among Christian servicemen and servicewomen, "If, for any reason, you find yourself at the Tokyo United States Army Hospital, look up Percy and Roy Kooshian. They are believers and they will take special care of you." We met several new friends through that network. Soon our lives were enriched by invitations from missionaries who invited us into their homes whenever we had time off from our hospital duties.

God richly answered our prayers by filling our lives with the friendships formed during those months in Japan, some of which have lasted over a lifetime. Truly, God is "Jehovah Jireh" (God Will Provide)!

6

Desperate Vow
October 1967

My twin brother and I had spent almost twenty-two months in the U.S. Army, fourteen months in Japan. There, in our permanent duty station, we served as surgical technicians in the operating suite of the Tokyo United States Army Hospital. But, while the army occupied our lives and duty at the hospital was always challenging and interesting, my spiritual life was in crisis.

We both had grown up in a church that taught us that sharing faith in Christ with others was more of an obligation than it was the natural result of an overflow of joy at being forgiven of our sins. Consequently, as a believer I felt guilty that I had never been successful in introducing someone to the Lord Jesus. I looked forward to the pastoral ministry, but one thought nagged me, "How could I hope to lead others to Christ if I was not involved in doing it now? After all, how could I become my ideal self in the future, if I was not moving toward that ideal self in the present?"

While that thought was ever-present in my mind, the months sped by in Japan. Observing society around me, I became more and more convinced that there were many unsaved men and women in uniform. However, few of them seemed to be receptive to spiritual things.

As the time approached for our term of duty to expire in three months, I became more desperate to break out of my prison of spiritual fruitlessness. The situation became so desperate that one day I prayed, "Lord, I will choose to be separated from active duty here and remain in Japan unless I am able to lead at least one person to the Lord." It was a desperate and radical statement from several points of view. However, I did not consider the huge challenge of finding a civilian job to support me in this country with such a foreign culture compared to mine. Nor did the practical questions as to food and lodging cross my mind. I had enjoyed, almost unconsciously, the basic support of the military. All I knew at the time was my desperate spiritual condition. How could I look forward to the ministry of leading people to faith in Christ if I were not doing so now? The issue was so personal that I could not even look to my twin brother, who was serving in the military with me, for support and counsel. The pressure was building within me as the days sped by, approaching my reassignment from Japan to stateside,

The answer came one day in an unexpected way. With a three-day pass from the hospital, I left the barracks to visit with some missionary friends. It was there that I found sensible advice. My host asked, "Why don't you talk to some of the Japanese students that visit the Chapel Center and just ask them if they had ever considered becoming a Christian?" The Chapel Center was a campus of buildings where Christian services were held. On Saturday nights, Japanese youth mingled with other young people, both military and civilian, who had gathered together for a youth Christian service. Many of the Japanese youth hoped to improve their English language skills by engaging American servicemen and women in conversation.

That Saturday night, following the chapel service, I approached the refreshment table laden with cookies and punch. While lifting a glass of punch, I glanced about and noticed a Japanese young man standing beside me. After offering him a glass of punch I introduced myself and asked him his name. In slightly accented English he replied, "My name is Yoshihiro Suginame." I commented on his linguistic proficiency and asked him, "Where did you learn to speak English so well?" He smiled modestly as he replied, "I was taught English at a missionary school." "Oh," I responded, "Are you a Christian?" He shook his head. "No, I am not." Mustering my confidence, I asked, "Do you know what a Christian is?" I was surprised by his answer. "Yes, I do." I paused, inwardly reviewing the progress of this strange conversation. The young man before me did not seem hostile to the idea of Christianity. Yet he was not a believer. Further, he professed to know what a Christian was. Relying on my Sunday school education, I reviewed the essentials of the Gospel with him, emphasizing the need to acknowledge personal sin and total surrender to Christ. He was familiar with all of it.

When I pressed the conversation further by asking, "Would you like to become a believer," he smiled eagerly and responded, "Yes! Yes, I would."

In the moments that followed, I reviewed the essentials of the Gospel once again. I concluded, "So the Bible says that God loves us and that Jesus died to pay the penalty for our sins." Then I quoted John 3:16, "For God so loved the world, that he gave his only begotten Son, that whosoever believeth on him should not perish, but have everlasting life." When we bowed in prayer, he confessed that he was a sinner in need of forgiveness and then surrendered his life to Christ.

Inwardly rejoicing, I welcomed him into the family of God. After agreeing to meet the following week at the Chapel Center, we parted. I saw him once again the next week. He was a changed person, with the joy of a true believer in Christ. Our visit this time was as brothers in Christ, and he expressed his appreciation for our encounter a week earlier. When we parted that evening, not only had we exchanged our contact information but we had set up a time to meet regularly for some basic Bible study together.

Unfortunately, I never saw him again. Unexpectedly, with only two days' notice, both Roy and I were shipped home and separated from active duty. The hospital needed two reliable technicians to tend to the needs of two men who had been paralyzed in separate accidents and needed care at a facility in Hawaii. Since Roy and I were near the end of our tour of duty, we were selected for early release from the military. Consequently, after being cleared for separation from our duty in the Far East, we journeyed home, releasing our patients to the medical team which met us in Hawaii. In a few more days we were released from active duty and were on our way home.

I wondered what would become of the young man who had accepted Christ just over two weeks before. Since we would not get to meet regularly for Bible study, I wondered if he would drift away from his spiritual experience. I wrote to him apologizing for the sudden departure, over which I had no control. Hoping to encourage him, I suggested that he attend the Tokyo Evangelical Church, where Roy and I had enjoyed such rich fellowship. Assuring him of my prayers, I signed the letter and posted it.

Two weeks later a letter arrived at our home from Japan, addressed to me. The return address had the name of Yoshihiro Suginame. He was writing his eternal thanks for my introducing him to the Lord Jesus. He mentioned that he attended the church which I had suggested and that he was pleased to meet fellow believers. One sentence in his letter pierced my heart. In his broken English he wrote, "You were God to me." I understood what that meant. He was expressing his gratitude that I had been God's representative. And now he was rejoicing in his eternal destiny.

While I was delighted that he had found faith in Christ, the thought was not lost on me that God had answered my prayers. He knew that I would be separated from active duty long before I knew it and had brought this young man into my life in part to enable me to keep my vow.

7

Home for Christmas
December 1957

Our first Christmas away from home occurred while Roy and I were in the military. Drafted on February 6, 1956, we underwent three months of basic training at Fort Ord, California, three more months of advanced medical training at Fort Sam Houston just outside of San Antonio, Texas, one month of On the Job Training (OJT) at Fort Lewis just south of Tacoma, Washington, and the rest of our military service in the country of Japan at the largest U.S. Army hospital in the Far East. In the early weeks stretching into more than two months, we were limited to the hospital and our fellow soldiers at camp. Camp Burness was the housing facility for the rank and file of soldiers who worked alongside nurses and doctors at the hospital. However, after a time, we came into contact with Christian missionaries, youth from the Christian Academy of Japan (CAJ) and other servicemen and women through the Youth Gospel Hour at the Chapel Center complex almost adjacent to the Imperial Palace in the center of Tokyo.

One of our favorite places to visit was the home of Homer and Millie Kreps, field director and wife of the Conservative Baptist field of Japan. We knew Phyllis Kreps, a graduate of Westmont College in our class of 1955, now a teacher at CAJ. Phyllis's younger sister Judi was a high school student at the same school. Since both girls were very personable and attractive, Roy and I tried to spend as much time in their home as possible. Homer and "Aunt Millie" were the epitome of warmth and hospitality whenever we visited, so it was natural that we were invited to spend our first Christmas away from home with them. Fortunately, we were granted the time off from the hospital.

The girls awaited our coming in their pajamas to make us feel that we belonged to the family. We bought gifts for the family, and they in turn had some gifts for us as well. It was not like being at our own home with parents and family, but it was a wonderful gesture, and we enjoyed a lovely time with them.

After ten months, we faced another lonely Christmas away from home. Naturally, the Kreps invited us to spend Christmas with them again. However, our loneliness began to increase when several of our fellow workers in the hospital joyfully advertised (with some degree of ridicule for those of us less fortunate than they) that their terms of active duty were over and that they were preparing to leave the Far East to be separated from the Army in time to spend Christmas at home. Within a week, they were scheduled to board a troop ship and sail from Tokyo to San Francisco. From there they would be transferred to the Stockton, California Separation Center at Travis Air Force Base. Gleefully they anticipated being home for the holiday season. On their last day of duty, their elation at the thought of going home could not be contained. At every opportunity, they reminded those of us who remained that while we would be spending another Christmas away from home, they would be relaxing with family and friends, relishing their separation from the armed services. "So long, suckers!" they jeered as they completed their final work shift. "While you are still slaving here, we'll be home for Christmas." Laughing at those of us who envied them their anticipation of home, they disappeared out of the OR, eager to leave.

As a significant number of our fellow workers left for home, the hospital became a much lonelier place. New replacements came, young men and women whom we did not know. The familiar surgical teams were gone, and we had to readjust to new personnel. Some of the men were difficult to work with, making the Operating Room (OR) suite a colder place to work. Others were not as competent as practiced and experienced technicians. Even though they had supposedly undergone the same training as we, their comprehension seemed weak to those of us who had become accustomed to the different demands and expectations of the doctors and nurses. Our attention was constantly being divided between our duties on the surgical team and the constant questions of the new members of the team.

Late in the afternoon on a day early in November of 1957, Roy and I were summoned into the office of the officer in charge of the OR. Major Davis glanced at us for a moment. She had given us the highest performance ratings possible for the quality of our work in the Operating Room Suite in the past.

She announced gravely, "I really hate to lose you boys from our surgical teams. You have really done a great job here. However," she paused, "two men need to be evacuated to Tripler U. S. Army Hospital in Honolulu, Hawaii. I am recommending that you two accompany these men on a Military Air Transport Service (MATS) flight home. A C-130 Hercules hospital plane will be leaving Tachikawa Air Base at 0700 hours, 48 hours from now." A smile lit her features. "I am also recommending that you receive orders to continue on from Hawaii to Travis Air Force Base to be separated from active duty. If you can clear Armed Forces Far East (AFFE) in the next two days, it is entirely possible that you both could be home for Christmas. Will you accept the assignment?"

Neither Roy nor I could hide our enthusiasm as we gratefully accepted her offer. Major Davis concluded, "You are hereby relieved of all duty except to clear AFFE. Please report to the hospital personnel office for a folder of all the necessary forms and papers to be completed and filed, along with a list of all the offices of the First Cavalry Division and AFFE, whose stamps will be required. Good luck." As we turned to leave, she added, "By the way, I am giving you boys the highest rating for duty performance. It will be entered into your military records. You did a great job!" We had 48 hours to be processed from AFFE, a procedure that usually took over a week to accomplish. However, we were determined to catch the MATS flight that left in two days.

Our first call was to the orthopedic ward, where we met our two patients lying on Stryker frames. A Portuguese fisherman had broken his neck in a fall on the slippery deck of a trawler, fishing off the coast of Japan in a storm. He wore a "halo" to stabilize his neck and spine. The other patient was a U.S. Marine who had been injured on a training exercise while in the Philippine Islands. He had broken his back. Both men were paralyzed from the neck down. During take-offs and landings of the huge aircraft, these men would need stabilization and careful attention to prevent further damage to their already severe injuries. During the long flight, they would also require some medical treatment. It was obvious to Roy and me that our flight from Tokyo to Honolulu would require our best medical skill to maintain the safety of our patients. We were informed that the landing at Midway Island required a steep bank and could possibly be rough due to inclement weather. The landing in Hawaii would be fairly smooth but with a u-turn to line us up with the runway at Hickam Field.

We spent the next 48 hours without sleep. During the daylight hours, we went from office to office in military installations all over the city of Tokyo, acquiring the proper stamps and signatures required to separate us from active service. At night we packed...all night long. With only a few daylight hours left, we called the Kreps and bade them "goodbye."

At 0500 hours on the day of departure, we loaded our two charges into the ambulances assigned to us and made the trip from the hospital in the center of Tokyo to Tachikawa Air Force Base on the outskirts of the city just in time to catch the flight.

The huge aircraft towered above us as we accompanied the Stryker frames of our patients into the cavernous but crowded body of the plane. Inside, we saw that on each side of the plane were three tiers of bunks along the sides from the front of the plane to the back. Reclining on the bunks were servicemen with urgent medical needs. Several nurses, medical flight attendants and technicians attended to the needs of the injured, sick and wounded men on the bunks. Roy and I escorted our two patients to an open area on the floor of the aircraft, where the Stryker Frames were attached to the floor, securing them from shifting as the plane ascended, banked and descended in the normal course of flight. Elevated a foot or so above the floor, the height of the Stryker Frames allowed the tension weights attached to the "halos" to hang free without the possibility of bumping into any impediment.

At 0700 the huge ramp at the back of the aircraft swung up, closing access to the plane. The loading ramp had now become part of the body. As the engines revved up for takeoff, we attended to the needs of our two patients. One of our main responsibilities was to brace the weights during takeoffs and landings, preventing undue strain on the "halo's" attached to the skull of each patient. The added pull of a swinging weight upon the already severe injuries of our patients could result in further spinal injury and even death. The huge plane began to slowly lumber down the runway. It gained speed so gradually that I feared we would reach the end of the runway before we lifted off. Seated in an area without windows we felt our anxiety mount as each second ticked by. Suddenly the vibrations of the wheels on a rough runway disappeared as the C-130 struggled to gain altitude for the long flight eastward over the Pacific Ocean. Soon we were high above the clouds, sunshine flooding the interior through the row of windows. The first leg of the flight proved to be smooth and uneventful as we attended to the comfort and safety of our patients.

Toward evening, the steady pitch of the engines changed as the large aircraft banked rather sharply, making its final approach to Midway Island. Roy and I had ministered to the needs of our patients some time before as the announcement had come over the loudspeakers for all personnel to secure for landing. The voice from the cockpit announced that we would layover for an hour while the plane was serviced for the next leg of the trip. Soon we were down on the runway of the U.S.

airbase at Midway Island. A welcome draft of fresh air flowed into the aircraft as the huge tail ramp lowered. Making sure that our patients were comfortable, Roy and I deplaned to spend a short time on the ground.

Not moving far from the parked aircraft because of our concern for the men who were dependent upon us, Roy and I marveled as we stared through the palm trees between the runway and the sandy beach at the magnificent sunset spreading vivid colors in the sky through which we had so recently flown. Midway was a historic place. Out in those waters underneath the colorful sunset, the determining battle of World War II in the Pacific had taken place 14 years before. With the peacefulness of the darkening evening, it was difficult to imagine that the water surrounding this tiny island was the site of horror and death for so many sailors and airmen on both sides of the conflict.

As the refueled plane rose into the eastern night sky some time later, the longest leg of our journey began. Throughout the night, as the plane droned steadily eastward, Roy and I tended to the needs and comfort of our patients in the darkened cabin.

Dawn streaked the sky as we approached the emerald green dots of the Hawaiian Islands 30,000 feet below. Descending steadily, the plane banked and landed smoothly at our destination, historic Hickam Field, which had suffered the treacherous attack of Pearl Harbor on December 7, 1941. The first two patients allowed off the plane were our men on Stryker frames. Their injuries were so grave and severe that they were given priority as they were rushed to Tripler Army Hospital. Roy and I bade them "good luck" as we parted. We had permanently signed off on the transport of our patients. Now they were the responsibility of Tripler Army Hospital, a few miles north and west of the air field.

Because of our extreme fatigue, Roy and I slept, ate and slept again in a constant cycle of fatigue for the entire 48-hour layover. We did not leave Hickam Field to explore the island, even though we were offered an automobile by an officer nurse who had worked with us in Tokyo some months earlier. Our flight to California, two days later, was much more comfortable without having medical responsibilities as we flew on a conventional airplane designed primarily to transport personnel.

Our arrival at Travis Air Force Base was unpretentious. As the only two men in our separation cycle, we escaped the expected regimentation which usually faced a much larger body of soldiers being discharged. Clutching our manila envelopes containing our papers, we reported to the Officer of the Day, who assigned us a place to sleep, pointed us to the mess hall, and told us to report to the appropriate building at 0800 for processing.

Two days later, the process was complete, and we firmly grasped our new manila envelopes containing our separation papers as we waited outside the headquarters building for military transportation to take us to the nearest greyhound bus station.

As we waited, we heard the tramping of marching feet. A large company of men rounded the corner and were brought to a halt almost in front of us. They were the next cycle of men to be separated from active duty in the army, standing at ease as the sergeant conferred with an officer regarding their housing. Suddenly we heard our names being called from some of the group. They were our former colleagues from Tokyo Army Hospital. "What are you guys doing here?" a voice called out. We waved our manila envelopes and shouted, "We are civilians now." "How did you get here before us? You weren't on the ship, too, were you?" they asked incredulously. They had sailed home by ship, an arduous voyage that had taken many days. We answered "We flew…all the way. It was a great trip with a layover in Hawaii." We did not explain that our "layover" merely comprised sleep and food. "Yeah, but how did you get out before us?"

At that moment, the sergeant called them to attention and marched them away toward their barracks. Their question was never answered.

Roy and I left the post a few minutes later, and with our prospects for a lonely second Christmas away from home erased, we boarded the military transportation headed for the local bus station. We were going home for Christmas!

As the hymn writer William Cowper penned in 1774, "God moves in a mysterious way His wonders to perform."

8

Seminary Preparation
September 1958

"Thou art my God. My times are in thy hand..." These words from David, the great king of Israel, in Psalm 31:14-15 began to impress themselves upon my consciousness during the years following my graduation from Westmont College. It happened this way.

Upon college graduation, our common aim was to attend a seminary with a view toward pastoral ministry. The mystery of identical twins arriving independently at the same life-changing conclusions may be explained by exact heredity and very similar environment. But I am convinced that there was a spiritual factor in this decision.

We had focused almost exclusively upon Fuller Theological Seminary in our home town of Pasadena, California. In our naïveté, we viewed the choice of seminaries simply as a matter of local availability, never realizing that such institutions of specialized learning were few and far between. We simply assumed that whichever graduate school was closest to our home was the logical one to attend. The subtle differences among seminaries totally escaped us.

Dallas Seminary (Dallas, Texas) was dispensational in its interpretation of the Bible. University of Chicago Divinity School (Chicago, Illinois) and Harvard Divinity School (Boston, Massachusetts) were theologically liberal at that time. Calvin Theological Seminary (Grand Rapids,

Michigan) was Christian Reformed. Northeastern Seminary (Rochester, New York) was Wesleyan. Oral Roberts University School of Theology (Tulsa, Oklahoma) was charismatic. Of course, we were vaguely familiar with the denominationally related schools -- Baptist, Presbyterian, Nazarene, Methodist, Church of Christ, Mennonite, Episcopal and Lutheran, to cite a few. Each school represented a different approach to biblical interpretation. Frankly, of those nuances of theological difference among the various institutions and of the other complex factors (location, tuition, academic standing, etc.) we were totally unaware.

Following our college graduation from Westmont College in 1956, we applied for the fall semester at Fuller Theological Seminary, just three miles from our home. The swift denial of our applications came in the mail, informing us that Westmont was an unaccredited school and that Fuller Theological Seminary standards allowed them to consider the applications of only the top two academic students of the graduating class from any unaccredited educational institution. In our ignorance, we did not realize that we were applying to one of the finest seminaries in the nation, rated in the top ten academic institutions of their kind. Since Westmont College was not yet accredited, we clearly did not qualify for entrance to Fuller.

Our keen disappointment was further affected by the prospect that if we did not attend school in the fall, we would be eligible for the draft and would spend at least the next two years in a military uniform. Employment was doubtful, for few employers would consider the expense of training personnel who could be called to military duty at the whim of the government. Without the prospect of school in the fall and the uncertainty of securing any type of long-term employment, we were truly discouraged. A phone call to the draft board revealed that with our placement on their list of possible draftees, we could expect to be called into the U.S. Army within ten to sixteen months. They informed us that international developments affected the call-up of young men into the service.

After praying about the situation, consulting with our older brother and our parents, and assessing the alternatives, we struck upon the idea of volunteering our draft status. We could affect our own futures by initiating our own conscription, thus saving us the time that would be spent in uncertainty, awaiting the inevitable call to military service. For with the draft hanging over our heads, we could not secure employment or be certain of acceptance into any graduate school.

When we contacted the local draft board again, we asked if there was a possibility of our being called into military duty immediately. We were surprised to learn that under federal regulations, the best that they could do, given their parameters, was to draft us in February of the coming year, some eight months away.

Those eight months of "idleness" were spent doing odd jobs for minimal pay. Nevertheless, we were impatiently looking toward the next chapters of our lives. In the period between graduation and military service, we learned that the draft was not simply an interruption of God's leadership in our lives but rather part of God's work in our lives. We were encouraged to view it as one of the necessary steps in the will of God.

As it turned out, we spent just a little over 22 months in the active military. Our assignments took Roy and me from California to Texas, on to Washington State, and finally to our main assignment in Tokyo, Japan. At each step of the way, our experiences matured us both physically and spiritually. Mentally we gained confidence as we were trained in the medical field to ultimately become surgical technicians in the main U.S. Army hospital in the Far East. Although we both were intrigued by the intricacies of being part of the surgical team during our time at the hospital, our common goal of seminary never left us.

Following our discharge from the army, we reapplied for admittance to Fuller Theological Seminary, hoping that we might be accepted. The letter which we received in response to our application stated that Fuller Seminary's policy of accepting only the top two students from unaccredited colleges remained unchanged. However, Westmont College had received accreditation in June of 1956, retroactive for two years. Since our graduation had occurred in June of 1955, the retroactive accreditation covered our diplomas. We were now graduates of an accredited Christian college. Therefore, Fuller Theological Seminary was glad to welcome us as students beginning in the fall semester of 1958. We graduated from Fuller Seminary four years later with two master's degrees each, one in Divinity and the other in Christian Education.

In retrospect, we could see that during our military tenure, the Lord was preparing the way for us to attend seminary in the same town where we lived, making it possible for us to live at home, work locally, and graduate from a prestigious graduate school. Those two years in the U.S. Army were not an interruption of God's will for our lives but part of His perfect will to enable us to attend seminary.

While we were not conscious of it, God was fulfilling His promise to meet our needs in His good time.

9

Girl of My Dreams
June 1960

After having been absent from our home church in Pasadena, California for almost two years, my twin brother Roy and I returned from active military duty. We had been stationed in Japan for over 16 months following 6 months in basic and advanced training. Our days as surgical technicians in the United States Army were at an end. We were relieved to be out of the military and able to pursue our much-anticipated seminary education. We had fulfilled our active duty at the end of November 1957, but not until the fall of 1958 did we begin seminary as first year students. At the time of our entrance to Fuller Seminary, we did not know that we would be spending four years there in the process of gaining two masters degrees each. Practically speaking, that meant that Roy and I would be attending Immanuel Baptist Church, our home church, for all of those four years. After a few Sundays at our home church, we were asked by the Christian Education Director to show some of our photography slides of Japan to the youth group of the church. We were glad to do so, relishing our time with the small group of high school students. What we did not know was that we were being observed and evaluated by members of the Christian Education commission with a view toward youth leadership.

Before long the pastor of the church and the Christian Education director approached us with the idea of becoming the youth leaders for the senior high school group. Since Roy and I needed a practical ministry experience along with our seminary classes, we accepted the challenge of supervising a group of about 15 youth.

A newly married couple, Dennis and Beth Orr, were to be co-sponsors with us. As the pastor and the Christian Education director outlined our responsibilities, we became aware that we were facing a challenging ministry. With our commitment to leadership training, we began to assign to different young people various responsibilities for conducting the youth meetings each Sunday evening. One person would lead the singing. Another would direct a pre-printed Bible study after being prepared to do so by the co-sponsors. Another would read Scripture. Still another would play the piano. Another might bring an object lesson, lead in prayer, read a sacred poem or present the "ministry of music," a solo, duet or instrumental offering. All of this was led by the youth under the watchful supervision of Dennis, Beth, Roy and me.

Within a matter of a month's time, it became clear to us that a fundamental flaw threatened the success of this church youth ministry. As youth leaders, we met each week to assess the direction and dynamics of the group. It became clear to us that a few of the boys were not taking the youth group seriously. Constantly harassing the girls who took a part in leading the group sessions, their taunts finally led to a crisis when two of the girls leading the group, burst into tears of frustration and fled the room. It was time to take action. Dennis Orr had just been released from the U.S. Navy. He, Roy and I still had the echoes of military discipline ringing in our ears, so we confronted the trouble makers, urging them to be kind and considerate toward the girls in the group. However, two boys from a broken family rejected our counsel. Although they sullenly heard us out, they did not change their abusive behavior of derision and rudeness whenever a girl took a position of leadership in the youth group sessions. After consulting together, Dennis, Roy and I made it clear following the next meeting that these two boys had a choice. They could either "shape up or ship out!"

Perhaps this was not the most tactful type of leadership, for the two boys refused to come to church any longer, angering their mother. Enraged by our ultimatum against her two boys, she complained to the Christian Education director. When confronted, we adamantly defended ourselves, stating that we had taken a hard line with the boys because they had shown disrespectful behavior toward the girls in the group. To our encouragement, we were supported by the Christian Education director, though the two boys and their mother angrily left the church. While we deeply regretted this failure in our own leadership, we noticed a change in the group. With the two troublemakers gone, the youth group began to grow. A new attitude of unity became evident. New boys began to come, attracted by the girls. Before long 30-40 young people were part of the Immanuel Baptist Church Youth Group. Then, sadly, Dennis and Beth moved away, leaving Roy and me in charge of the group. To balance out the leadership, the church asked a tall, beautiful girl to serve on the leadership team. Roy, Norma and I got along very well, meeting weekly to assess the course and progress of the youth group. We set curriculum, counseled youth, organized trips and social activities, and generally made ourselves accessible to the youth.

Although Roy and I were older than the group by 10 years, we were not unaware of the uncommon beauty and grace of many of the girls in the group. Some were stunningly beautiful. However, we took our responsibilities very seriously and considered these young people to be our younger "brothers and sisters." Our charge was to protect, nurture and love in a parental way. Our primary purpose was to disciple them into mature Christian adulthood.

One of the girls whom I noticed immediately was a rather slender girl with a shy, winning smile. She was a junior in high school. But I considered Carolyn Howie, with all the other girls, to be strictly "off limits," not only because of her age but because our purpose was to be Christian role models and spiritual leaders for all the youth under our care. Carolyn seemed to be a responsive believer, participating in the group as much as her reserved and quiet spirit would allow. I automatically viewed her as I did all the girls in the group -- someone to be considered as a spiritual responsibility. Although she was very attractive, I viewed her as a member to be protected, nurtured and befriended.

Within two years, she had graduated from high school and had begun her college education, still somewhat shy and retiring, yet graceful and friendly. That year, because our Christian Education director and his family were called to another church, I was asked to assume the position of "Part-Time Youth Director" in the absence of a Christian Education director. My responsibilities included the oversight of the advisors of all three youth groups -- junior high, high school and college.

Whenever I had occasion to call upon the Howies, particularly when dating Carolyn's cousin who was living with them at the time, I could not help but take notice of Carolyn. One evening when visiting the Howie home, I gave a slight tug on Carolyn's blond curl as she sat in an upholstered chair facing away from where I stood. I thought, "Lord, why couldn't I marry a beautiful girl like this one?" It was almost a fleeting thought, not really considered a possibility, given how beautiful and sought-after she was and how plain and ordinary I considered myself to be. However, I didn't realize until much later that the Lord had clearly heard what I considered to be an unattainable wish.

At that time I was also involved in the church choir under the direction of a gifted musician, Tom Fox, who with his wife Barbara made an awesome musical team. Barbara was an accomplished organist, complementing the musical talents of her husband.

At choir one evening Tom announced a drive for new choir members. He informed us that we were having a choir banquet and that we were encouraged to invite others to the event. The Crusader's Quartet in which I sang with Roy, Jerry Hudlow and Chuck Emert agreed to do its part by inviting four girls to the banquet. We would not really be "dating" them because we were all going together as a group. As we considered which girls to invite, I thought of Carolyn. I made it clear to her that this was not a "date," for although she was in college, I considered her too young for me to date. Even with those terms, she accepted my invitation.

When I announced to the rest of the quartet that Carolyn had agreed to join me, one by one they sadly admitted that they had been turned down. I was now on my own with a girl nine years my junior. With some embarrassment, I called upon Carolyn's mother and explained that I did not intend to "date" her daughter, for we were supposed to be a part of a group, but the others had dropped out. Her smiling reply startled me. "It's o.k. with me, Percy. Enjoy yourselves!" Still feeling a little edgy and not a little hesitant, I escorted Carolyn to the choir banquet. The evening was not a total success, for while Carolyn decided to join the choir, she was not all that impressed with me that evening. I, in turn, did not think that she was my type. So when I condescended to ask her out on a "real" date two weeks later, I was shocked when she turned me down for no apparent reason. A third attempt on my part for a date succeeded, however, only after a serious and somewhat desperate effort on my part to persuade her to accept my invitation. On that third date we discovered that our first impressions of each other were not fully accurate. We eventually learned that we shared a variety of common interests.

Dating began and courtship ensued; two years later we were married. As newlyweds, we began our life together in the ministry of Christian Education. God blessed us with three children, all of whom are believers and are sincerely following the Lord. Carolyn has been an excellent wife and mother, a gracious hostess and an ideal "pastor's wife."

The Lord, who knew what I needed even though I was unsure at the beginning, brought the perfect partner into my life, proving once again the validity of His promise to meet all our needs.

10

Children, Cars, and Color T.V.

February 1963

It was one of those perplexing, unanswered questions that occupied my mind at the time and overshadowed the real issues surrounding me. Why was it that I, who had witnessed many cesarean deliveries and an actual natural birth during my service in a military hospital, was not allowed to see the birth of my own children? I had already witnessed the birth of babies to patients whom I did not know personally. It would seem only reasonable that I should be permitted to witness the birth of my own children. But it was not to be. The reason given by physicians and hospitals at the time related to insurance coverage. "Unauthorized persons" were not permitted in the delivery rooms of the local hospitals. Insurance would not cover any damages occurring in a delivery room if non-hospital personnel were present. However, I felt that my experience as a surgical technician in the service of my country should have exempted me from such restrictions. Preoccupied with this issue, I missed the importance of the greater circumstance.

As newlyweds, Carolyn and I desired to start a family. (Because of my age, we decided to embark on parenthood as early as possible.) Our discussions regarding the creation of a family centered primarily upon my age. At the age of thirty, I did not look forward to dealing with a possibly rebellious teenager while I was in my mid-to-late fifties. So, we began the pleasant task of procreation. Any misgivings I may have harbored regarding my competency as a parent were somewhat offset by the cheerful, optimistic, willing, cooperation of my young and beautiful wife. What immediately troubled me were the rising costs of delivery and hospital care. Our limited income did not allow us to cover the cost of having more than one child, and even then, we would have to exercise extreme frugality if we were to afford the costs of childbirth.

As a youth pastor, I had taught Bible classes on the names of God including *Jehovah Jireh* (God will provide). Both Carolyn and I believed that God could supply all our needs, yet, a lingering doubt nagged at me as I calculated the costs of having a child, measured by our limited resources. Hospital fees were not the only expenses, for outfitting a room with furniture and supplies represented a formidable financial outlay.

But the practical outworking of God's provision proved to be as marvelous as it was surprising.

Dr. George Brown and his beautiful wife, Lee, were members of our church, the First Baptist Church of La Mesa, California. Their lovely daughter was a part of the youth of the church. Not familiar with the busy schedule of this very popular physician and of his singular fame and accomplishments, we gravitated toward him simply because he was a member of our church. So it seemed natural to adopt him as our family doctor. However, as time progressed, we became more aware of his stature in our community and of his remarkable accomplishments.

During his college years, George Cummings Brown played football for the Naval Academy in Annapolis, Maryland, quickly earning academic and sports honors. Respected as an All-American, he was later inducted into the Football Hall of Fame. A decorated Naval officer, he served honorably during World War II both on surface ships and in the Submarine Service. Following the end of the war, he attended Johns Hopkins Medical School to ultimately receive his medical degree.

After establishing his practice in El Cajon, California, Dr. Brown founded a free medical clinic at the San Diego Rescue Mission and regularly donated his time to the courteous treatment of the homeless men and women who were in desperate need of medical care. He treated them as if they were the highest paying patients among his clientele.

For fifteen years he was the team physician for the San Diego State College Aztec football team. He also began a relief ministry for local indigent people. When Carolyn and I arrived at the church to begin our ministry there, Dr. Brown was already serving as the chairman of the San Diego Medical Society.

Despite his prominent standing in the community of San Diego, Dr. Brown was a humble Christian. Acquainted with our economic limitations, he declined to charge us for his services when he delivered our first two children. We also received regular medical care for our family without charge. God provided this remarkable man to help meet our needs.

His wife, Lee, was equally kind and generous. One might have suspected that a beautiful and cultured wife of a prominent physician would be remote and reserved, but she was not. Even when her husband was called away on a Sunday because of a medical emergency, she was faithfully in church. Her generosity became evident to me early on in my ministry at the First Baptist Church of La Mesa.

The church had a vital youth ministry, both to junior high and senior high young people. Sunday school, evening youth meetings, and weekly projects kept the youth engaged in Christian instruction and service. Twice a year, our youth counsellors and Carolyn would help plan special campout weekends for our church youth. Transportation to distant destinations was always a challenge, but supportive adults in the church volunteered to drive their vehicles loaded with youth to the selected place. Lee Brown was not free to drive her new car but was willing to loan it to the church whenever we needed it, most a generous gesture. We were always in need of cars and drivers to help transport our youth since the church did not have a bus or van.

One day, while in my office in the annex of the church, the phone rang. Lee Brown was on the other end of the line. After greeting me and exchanging pleasantries, she came to the point of her call. "I am planning to buy a new car and wondered if you would help me choose the type of vehicle that would help support the transportation needs of our youth." Dumbfounded, I stammered, "You want me to help you choose a car?" "Yes," she answered breezily "I would like to choose one that will help you transport youth to your various activities. You, or a church adult, could drive it to conferences. What model would you like me to purchase?" Recovering, I answered, "A nine-passenger station wagon would be nice. it would have a greater capacity to hold youth." As if the decision had just been made, Lee ended the call, "Thank you. That is the car I will buy. Whenever you need it, just call me, and we will make the arrangements."

Mrs. Brown was true to her word. The next youth weekend conference was rapidly approaching. When we arranged for transportation for our youth, Lee Brown's new station wagon was one of the first vehicles to be scheduled. An adult volunteer was glad to drive to Mount Palomar and back in the luxurious comfort of her car. God was meeting our needs through the generosity of the Brown family.

Not long after, Dr. George Brown called at our house on a Saturday night. "I hate to bother you, but are you interested in a color television set?" Without waiting for an answer, he continued, "I apologize for its condition, for it isn't working very well, so I had to replace it with a newer set. Would you be interested in this old set? If so, I could bring it around tomorrow afternoon. Again, I apologize for its condition. I don't know how long it will last, but if you are interested, I would be glad to drop it off at your house. It won't cost you anything." He paused with a hopeful note in his voice. Carolyn and I did not have a television set at all. Considering our household budget, even an inexpensive set was out of our financial reach. (Our finances simply did not permit such a luxury.) Naturally, we readily accepted Dr. Brown's offer.

Following the church service the next day, Dr. Brown lugged a huge square box into our living room. It was about twenty-four inches wide, twenty-four inches tall, and eighteen inches deep. In comparison with the size of black and white models, it ranked among the largest. In eager anticipation, Carolyn and I had prepared a small table in the corner of the living room to support the set. It was obvious by Dr. Brown's exertion of effort that the set was very heavy. This was confirmed as Carolyn and I later adjusted the position of the set. By the time Dr. Brown left our house, it was time for the evening service to begin. Hurriedly Carolyn and I prepared to leave the house for church. However, just as a test, I turned on the television set to sample the quality of the picture. After a few moments of warming up, a spectacular picture emerged on the screen of snow-capped mountains above the deep blue waters of a lake, upon which floated a brilliant red boat. Two men in brightly colored clothes were idyllically fishing. It was a picture that burned itself into my mind as we turned off the set and rushed away to the evening service at our church.

Through this generous and kind family, God provided much more than our daily needs. But their generosity did not end there. Long after we had moved to another church, the benevolence of Dr. and Mrs. Brown followed us.

After almost four years in La Mesa, Carolyn and I had accepted a call from the First Baptist Church of The Dalles, Oregon in 1967. We were in our second year of ministry there when one afternoon we received a phone call. On the other end of the line Dr. Brown's confident voice inquired, "My daughter Lonnie and I are flying up through the Pacific Northwest. We would like to visit you, and stay overnight before resuming our trip. Would you be free to host us?" Ascertaining the projected day and time of our visit, I responded, "We would be glad to have you as our overnight guests. However, I have a hospital call in Portland scheduled for that morning and would be able to visit only for an hour or so, before driving the two-hundred-mile round trip to the hospital and back." His reply was typical of his magnanimity.

"Lonnie and I are flying my own plane. We could fly you to the Portland International Airport, rent a car there, and drive to the hospital. We could return the same way, and complete our visit before continuing our trip. Is that satisfactory with you?" After stammering my stunned agreement, we ended the call.

As it turned out, everything proceeded exactly as planned. On the appointed day, Dr. Brown and his daughter flew into the Dallesport air field just across the river. We were there to greet them. Following an afternoon tour of The Dalles, consumption of one of Carolyn's tasty dinners, and a leisurely evening visit, we retired.

The next morning, Carolyn and I packed our children into the car and drove our guests across The Dalles bridge to the Dallesport air field. It was a clear morning as Dr. Brown, Lonnie and I entered the plane and strapped ourselves in. After communicating with air traffic control, Dr. Brown expertly piloted the plane down the compacted gravel runway into the cool morning air. As the plane rose, Dr. Brown banked, pointing the nose of the plane in a westward direction toward Portland. Looking downward as the overhead wing dropped, I could see Carolyn and the children waving to us. Soon we were on our way down the Columbia River Gorge to Portland.

What appeared at ground level as a mighty river now seemed a modest ribbon of water. Considered one of the seven natural wonders of the modern world, the Columbia River Gorge lived up to its designation in the morning light. It was a view that few have seen. The higher altitudes of commercial flights do not afford the up-close view of the gorge's many wonderful details. Seeing the towns and communities dotting the banks of the great river from an altitude just above the rim of the gorge was a once-in-a-lifetime experience. Looking down upon the gorge revealed natural wonders not apparent when viewed from the highway.

Glancing to the north, we could see the peaks of the Washington State Cascade volcanoes; Mt. Adams, Mt. St. Helens, and the other distant peaks of Mt. Rainier and Glacier Peak. On the Oregon side of the gorge rose the eleven thousand, two hundred fifty-foot peak of Mt. Hood. Further south we could see the peaks of Mt. Washington and Mt. Jefferson, the Three Sisters and Mt. Bachelor. It was a spectacular vista enjoyed only from a great height.

After a successful visit in the hospital, in the mid-afternoon light we returned to The Dalles, enjoying a different view of the same communities and mountain peaks that we had relished earlier that morning.

At the Dallesport airfield, Carolyn and our small children awaited us. As the small plane rolled to a stop, Dr. Brown explained that he and Lonnie would be moving on. There was enough daylight left to justify their flying on to their next destination in Washington.

Bidding Dr. Brown and Lonnie farewell, Carolyn and I, along with our children, waited by the car to see our friends depart. Once again, the engine roared as the plane gained speed down the runway and lifted into the sky. As the small plane ascended above the gorge and disappeared over the rim, we marveled again at the role that this family had played in our lives. They had cared for our family, assisted us in the ministry, and shared their benevolence with us. We never saw Dr. Brown or his wife again. However, the imprint of their magnanimity never paled in our minds.

God had used them not only to provide for our needs but also to encourage us in our ministry. Truly, God not only addresses our daily necessities but also enriches our lives with exceptional people and beautiful experiences.

11

Refrigerator Swindle
Spring 1966

The birth of our first child, Suzanne, brought great joy to our lives. Carolyn was a "natural" when it came to child care and an ideal mother. Our second child, Catherine, was also a great delight. We were blessed with two beautiful little children. However, Catherine's birth coincided with a problem in our household infrastructure.

Our apprehension quotient arose as we realized that our old second-hand refrigerator had finally died -- and this on the day before Carolyn and Catherine were due to come home from the hospital. The appliance's failure was a matter of age and condition. The compressor had finally stopped functioning. The prospect of replacing the 20-year-old compressor was totally impractical, for a new part was too expensive to be placed in an aging unit. Faced without a means of cooling the milk necessary for the health of our children and the preservation of the perishables necessary for meals, we were desperate to obtain another refrigerator immediately. However, we could not afford a new unit because of the high prices commanded by appliance dealers. Our personal savings were very limited. The fact that it was summertime in Southern California made the necessity of cooling the supply of milk critical for our children, so we had reached a moment of crisis.

Motivated by the urgency of our need, we visited a nearby second-hand appliance store upon the recommendation of a local workman, who was modifying an apartment complex in our neighborhood. He seemed to be knowledgeable, so we took his recommendation without hesitation.

The next morning we drove to the recommended establishment. Ignoring the dilapidated appearance of the used appliance store, we entered with high hopes of finding a serviceable unit to replace our now defunct appliance. Sorting among the alternatives, we came upon a larger model with what we considered to be a reasonable price of $200. The shiny white enameled finish and the polished chrome trim attracted our attention. Upon closer examination, the spacious interior and special features seemed not only adequate for our needs but even a little luxurious. Draining our meager savings, we quickly agreed to pay the price, considering ourselves most fortunate to have discovered such a bargain, which included next-day delivery.

Slightly oversized, the refrigerator still managed to squeeze tightly into the allotted space in our small kitchen. For two days we rejoiced in our good fortune in finding such a jewel among the other worn appliances at the second-hand store. However, our joy was short-lived. After two days, we opened the refrigerator door only to find warm air spilling out of the unit. No longer did it cool the perishables we had stored there. Perplexed, we placed a call to the store to report the failure. The response was sympathetic, and we were assured that a repairman would be out the next day. It did not happen. A second call resulted in an apology on the part of the retailer and a promise that a representative would come to our house to evaluate the problem.

That also did not happen. In response to a third call, the appliance dealer offered to trade the old refrigerator for a used washing machine. Obviously, that did not meet our immediate needs, so we declined the offer.

Several times after that our calls for service were met with a cold response that our product had been sold in an "as-is" condition and that there was no recourse but for us to deal with some other appliance supplier.

In the meantime, our perishables (milk included) spoiled rather rapidly in the warm weather. Even an ice chest did not preserve these items with any effectiveness.

We then placed a call to the local Sears store, which sent out a repairman immediately. After examining our defective fridge, he concluded that it was a unit primed to last a week or two after the sale. His opinion was firm: we had been swindled.

When the original dealer refused to refund us any of the money that we had spent on his product, we called the Better Business Bureau, hoping to gain some leverage for financial redress. They virtually shrugged their corporate shoulders in a helpless admission that they were only a referral organization, not a law enforcement agency.

In desperation, we contacted the Sears dealer once again. He turned out to be a fine Christian man. After some research, he called us to offer us a small, pre-owned, ugly yellow refrigerator for $40, assuring us that it was a dependable unit. The color caused us to hesitate, but reasoning that "beggars can't be choosers," we accepted his offer.

The sturdy little, pre-owned refrigerator lasted for over twenty more years, dependably preserving whatever contents we entrusted to its care. Moreover, the freezer unit never failed, producing ice cubes as well as solidly freezing its contents without fail. Further, the unit survived several moves made during its lifetime with us. When the time finally came to replace it, we were in somewhat improved financial circumstances and were able to purchase a new refrigerator. As we sadly bade farewell to our ugly little yellow refrigerator, we recognized that it had lasted phenomenally longer than its engineers had originally envisioned. Truly, it was God's refrigerator, provided for us in our time of critical need.

12

Beyond All That You Can Ask or Think

January 1970

As my wife looked at the bare shelves which we had erected, made up of two stacks of cement blocks with thin planks of particleboard sandwiched between, erected for the storage of food items packaged for family consumption, she asked in anguish, "Where will we get any food? How will we feed our children?" It was a dire plight. At this juncture, the few cupboards in the kitchen of the modest rented duplex where we lived bravely held a few plates and table service but no edible goods. Our small second-hand refrigerator contained only the essentials to keep hunger at bay. A depressing silence hung heavily between us.

The church to which we had come just four weeks earlier was a small congregation meeting in a new church building, recently completed. However, the congregation was barely meeting the monthly mortgage payments and was in arrears on their obligations to pay for pulpit, pews and other church furniture. Further, the church was behind in its payment of utility bills, placing it in danger of having its water and electricity service shut off. The members of the church came mainly from the wood industry -- loggers, truckers, and mill workers. There were a few teachers, a couple of small business owners and several retired seniors who lived in the large subsidized high-rise housing in the middle of town.

The small logging community of Cottage Grove nestled in a tiny valley on the edge of the southern Oregon Mountains just south of Oregon's wide and fertile Willamette Valley. The Bohemia Mountains with two large lakes nearby offered beautifully scenic views and varied recreational opportunities for campers, boaters, hunters and fishermen. Naturally, during the short summer months, the population of Cottage Grove would swell as people from the larger cities of the Willamette Valley flocked to the more pristine settings of the nearby mountains, streams and lakes.

The attendance at the morning worship services of our small church consisted of about 40 people, including the children. However, in the first three weeks after our arrival, three elderly people died, and two other families stopped attending, further reducing our membership ranks. While Carolyn and I had fervently sought to follow the Lord, we now began to wonder if we had somehow missed His leading. The remaining congregation seemed to appreciate our coming, but resembled a lost flock of sheep gravitating toward the shepherd for security and leadership.

Our meager financial resources were gone, used up in the last three weeks to pay the moving costs and to keep our family barely fed. We had no cash reserves. In addition, during the first weeks of ministry in the new church, there had been no paycheck from the church. The treasurer avoided any mention of it, even though we thought the question of remuneration had been adequately addressed in one of our interviews with the pulpit committee.

We now had three small children for whom to care and feed. Carolyn was near tears. I was not far from them myself. Had we misunderstood the pulpit committee, which assured us that the church could support a pastor and his family? There was no apparent prospect of money or food in the immediate future. Our desperate plight was intensified by the fact that we were in a new community where we knew no one except the small church family we were just beginning to serve. We realized that we were dependent upon a church that was not fiscally sound.

Not knowing where else to turn, we bowed our heads in the kitchen and prayed for help. "Father, You called us here, and we will serve at Your leading. If we starve here, it will be Your responsibility because we are certain that You called us here, and we are not leaving until You lead us elsewhere. We thank You in advance for Your help. Amen."

Summoning up my nerve, I approached the church treasurer following the next worship service. He was a cheerful, friendly mill worker in his mid thirties with a wife and four children. They were one of the pillar families of the church. I began by asking rather naively, "When is the pay period here at the church?" He replied, "As soon as we get some money." I remembered that the church had been taking offerings in the morning worship services, so the next question was obvious. "What about the offerings that we are taking each week? What has become of them?" "Oh," he replied, "they go to pay the back bills." Stunned, I asked, "Back bills? What back bills?" "Oh yeah," the treasurer explained with a broad smile, "we've got plenty of those. As soon as we pay them off, we will get around to paying you."

I then asked a question whose answer left me further unnerved. "Is there a Finance Committee in the church?" "Nope, he replied, "I'm it. The people voted to authorize me to do all I can to keep the church financially afloat. And I'm doing the best I can. No one is helping me." And then he added rather sadly, "And we do not have any money to pay a pastor." I remonstrated, "But when we asked the pulpit committee that very question a couple of months ago, you assured us that the church could support a pastor with a small family like ours." He replied rather sheepishly, "Well yeah, I did say that, but if I had admitted the truth, you wouldn't have come." He nodded positively, "And we did want you to come." His response was hardly encouraging.

We arranged to meet the next day to review the financial records of the church. When I arrived at his home on Monday morning, I discovered that there were no financial records – none other than the check stubs in the church check book along with several shoe boxes full of receipts and financial notes written on scraps of paper. As we sifted through the check stubs and scattered receipts and papers, the financial picture that emerged was appalling. Church committees had accumulated bills on credit with various businesses, but the church had no ability to pay for expensive flowers for the sick, food for church socials, Sunday school supplies, and unexplained miscellaneous expenses. Further, the seven church missionaries, whose pictures were prominently displayed on a mission board in the narthex of the church, had not been supported financially for over 18 months. The church furniture (sanctuary pews, pulpit, choir-loft pews, communion-table, and modesty shields) had not been paid for. In fact, no payments had been tendered to our creditors in over a year. The church still owed several thousand dollars to a church furniture company, which was now dunning the church $50 a month penalty interest on the unpaid balance. It became clear that the church was rapidly going bankrupt.

The church treasurer and I immediately set some spending policies since the nominal boards of the church were virtually non-functioning. We arranged to meet each Sunday evening to prioritize the bills of the church to pay the most urgent past-due debts first. Carolyn met with us and advised us as to how much money our family would need for food and bills that week. We settled on an average of $25 a week to help us buy essential groceries. Still, Carolyn and I were deeply concerned. The financial picture for the church as well as for us was bleak indeed. We continued to pray for our desperate need of basic provisions.

One Sunday evening shortly after our initial meeting with the treasurer, we returned home following a sparsely-attended evening service. We had hardly settled down when the doorbell rang. Opening the door, we were met with a group of people carrying several large cardboard boxes of gaily wrapped items and groceries. When we asked the people who they were, they identified themselves as members of a sister Conservative Baptist church a few miles away in Dexter. Their pastor had heard of our plight and had motivated his congregation to take up a "pounding" (a pound of this or that) to help feed the pastor's family in Cottage Grove.

Each can, carton and package was gift-wrapped, and the whole effect was rather overwhelming. The boxes and bags seemed to overflow with good will. After brief, cheerful expressions of love and concern, the group from Dexter prayed with us in gratitude for God's provision. And as suddenly as this happy group had appeared at our doorstep, they departed, leaving us the pleasure of unwrapping our gifts of food and supplies.

After we said our "goodbyes," the children began to dance with excitement. Suzanne, our seven-year-old daughter, marveling at the overflowing boxes of gift wrapped items, asked, "Who sent us all this?" Confidently I reverted to my pastoral self and replied unctuously, "God did!" Her eyes squinted in suspicion. Struggling in her seven-year-old mind to make the connection between the spiritual and temporal worlds, she demanded, "How did He get it here?" As I realized that my glib theology would not satisfy her, I searched my mind for a more satisfactory answer. "Actually," I explained, "God put it in the hearts of those people to collect food and supplies and to bring it all to us." She nodded her head in a moment of silent contemplation and finally seemed satisfied with that explanation. I had no idea that the other children were listening.

Catherine, our four-year-old, was already tearing away the colorful paper from what turned out to be a box of oatmeal. Quickly losing interest in that box, she turned away to another item. Then Mark, our two-and-a-half year-old, quickly decided to investigate this flood of gifts, and soon all of us were excitedly tearing the gift wrappings from cans, packages, boxes and containers of all kinds and sizes.

Even though the moon was shining in the clear cold night, we could see that it was quite past the children's bed time. Again, we paused to thank the Lord for His bountiful provision before I gathered up the torn and wrinkled paper, the ribbon and the bows, pushing my way through the front door toward the trash can in the side yard by the corner of the garage. As I lifted the lid to press the paper down into the can, behind me I heard the front door slam as a little body ran out into the middle of the front lawn. It was Mark. Looking up into the sky, he shouted, "Thank you, God. You are a good God!" Shivering both from the cold and his excitement, he turned and ran back into the house. The spontaneous expression of childlike gratitude to God brought tears to my eyes as I witnessed in the darkness at the side of the house the unbridled joy and gratitude of my small son. Weeping with joy, I prayed, "Dear God, please keep my son as sensitive and grateful to You all of his life as he is at this moment."

Returning to the front room, I found Carolyn surveying all the groceries and food lying scattered on the floor. Then she asked a most significant question: "Where are we going to put it all? We simply do not have room enough in the kitchen for all of this!"

Within a few months, our church applied and received mission aid from the Conservative Baptist Fellowship. This augmentation of the pastor's salary continued, on a sliding scale, for three years, by which time the church had grown to be self-supporting. Within that time, the church paid all its back bills and operated in the black. In it all, we did not miss a meal or lack a payment on our utilities and other bills.

The provision was beyond our imagination. God had sent an unmistakable message to us of His faithfulness and love, expressed in the overwhelming provision of our needs.

"Now to him who is able to do immeasurably more than all we ask or imagine, according to his power that is at work within us, to him be glory in the church and in Christ Jesus throughout all generations, for ever and ever! Amen." Ephesians 3:20-21 (NIV)

13

Decision to Tithe
February 1970

For the first seven years of our marriage, Carolyn and I lived from paycheck to paycheck -- not because we were profligate in our spending, but because our income was very modest. The wages at the first church where I served as a Christian Education director were minimal, to say the least. Even by the then-current standards, ours was a miniscule yearly salary. The generous food shower which welcomed us to the church was encouraging, but when that was gone, our little family of four faced the challenge of economic survival. In my idealism, I had negotiated my salary package at the interview with the church board by saying, "You meet the needs of our family, and I will give myself wholeheartedly to the ministry of the Lord." Apparently, the church board interpreted that to mean that the church could save money by paying me the lowest possible salary. Our wages looked even smaller in the yearly printed budget compared to the senior pastor's salary. Our wages did not change significantly during that first ministry. Consequently, we gave small amounts of money to the church in an irregular and sporadic manner. It seemed to be more of a grudging payment of a debt rather than a joyful reminder of the grace and provision of God.

The second church where we served in The Dalles, Oregon paid us a little more, but the cost of living in that area was also much higher than in our former ministry. Nevertheless, we were thankful that we had lived without debt for the three and a half years there. However, as in our first ministry, we gave as much as we felt we could afford at the time. Three years later we left that ministry with no money in our bank account. Nor did we have any semblance of a retirement or pension plan. We were virtually penniless except for a monetary going-away gift from the church.

As we moved from The Dalles to Cottage Grove, our status changed from Christian Education director to pastor of the church. My wife and I hoped that the small salary negotiated with the church would be adequate for our growing family of three children, but within the first three weeks we learned that the church was virtually insolvent. Offerings barely paid the mortgage. Utility bills were in arrears. The church owed several thousand dollars for the church furniture. Of most significance to us was the fact that there was nothing left over from each weekly offering that could be applied to the support of the pastor and his family. While it lasted, we lived on the small "love gift" from our former church. When that ran out, I was compelled to approach the treasurer of the church with questions about the solvency of the church. In our interview, I learned the true financial condition of our small fellowship.

It was critical that the church family be motivated to give. However, my conscience convicted me that Carolyn and I had not been faithful in giving generously to the Lord over the past years of our church ministry in the field of Christian Education. As we talked together, Carolyn and I agreed that it would be hypocritical of us to ask the church members to give generously if we did not set the example first. We determined to start tithing immediately. God honored that decision, and the results for both our family and the church were dramatic. Within three years the church became financially independent.

Although our salary never rose to great heights, our family managed to operate a modest income. We spent money more conservatively. The landlords of the duplex where we lived were very generous and gracious, setting our rent at a low monthly rate. Twice our salary was reduced by

10% due to a national recession, but we continued to tithe faithfully. Gradually we came to realize that we were not giving to the church but to the Lord through the church. It soon became a joy to give more than the tithe.

We even began to contribute as a family to the support of some of our missionary friends. We were certainly enriched ourselves as our "family missionaries" came to visit us from time to time, staying with us and sharing their experiences of the mission field. We did not know at the time what a positive influence the exposure to missionaries would have upon our children. Two of our three children have served as missionaries in far distant places in Africa, Europe and the Middle East.

By the time our family left the church to move on to our next ministry, we owned two automobiles. One was an old used car, the other a station wagon which we had purchased new. Further, I had a few tools that allowed me to enjoy the pleasures of working with wood.

Several months after leaving the house in Cottage Grove, which we had been in the process of buying, we received a check for several thousand dollars upon the sale of that house. This enabled us to purchase another home in Oregon City. Prior to our retirement from the active pastorate, the mortgage was paid in full.

Clearly, the Lord had abundantly blessed our decision to tithe. We learned the truth of II Corinthians 9:7-9.

"Everyone must make up his own mind as to how much he should give. Don't force anyone to give more than he really wants to, for God only prizes cheerful givers. He is able to make it up to you by giving you everything you need and more so that there will not only be enough for your own needs but plenty left over to give joyfully to others. As the Scriptures say, 'The godly man gives generously to the poor. His good deeds will be an honor to him forever.'" (Living Bible)

14

Buy A Pew
March 1970

After serving in the field of Christian Education for over ten years, Carolyn and I felt the Lord calling us into pastoral ministry. While academically prepared for such a ministry, I was unprepared for the realities. Having been an associate in Christian Education for eight years, I served under the supervision of a senior pastor, who bore the total responsibility for the ministries in the church. But when Carolyn and I responded to a call to the pastorate of a small church in a little logging community in Oregon, the whole responsibility for ministry was mine and mine alone.

We left The Dalles, a small town on the banks of the Columbia River, one cold Saturday night in early December and drove almost two hundred miles through a severe snowstorm to the town where we would make our home for the next fifteen years. With limited visibility, we drove west through Portland and turned south into the Willamette Valley to the logging community of Cottage Grove, twenty miles south of Eugene. Even though we spent several hours making our way slowly through gusty winds and blinding snow, we arrived safely at our destination at 6:00 a.m. on our first Sunday of ministry. Rather exhausted, we still were grateful that our three small children had slept through most of the journey. Spending the next two hours in our unfurnished lodging, we rested and attended to the comfort of our children. Fortunately, in anticipation of our arrival, church members had obtained keys to our half of the duplex and made sure that the building's utilities were all functioning properly. As we hurried to prepare to meet our new church family, we left the borrowed truck loaded with our household items and drove our vehicle to church. We arrived in time for the Sunday services.

Located beside a large park-like field of mown grass, the church building was small but new, having been completed just under a year before our arrival. It was an attractive building with decorative stained-glass windows at the front of the sanctuary. The interior of the building with its social hall, Sunday school classrooms, restrooms and utility room was neat and clean. The carpet throughout the building bore silent testimony to its recent installation.

Warmly received by the church family, we were buoyed by our idealism as we faced the future of this ministry. It seemed like an ideal situation for my first pastoral ministry. Little did we anticipate that our idealistic optimism would soon be tempered in the fires of experience and reality.

On our first Monday morning, I discovered that the church office, a small fifteen-by-fifteen-foot room located on the southeast corner of the building, looking out on a quiet tree-lined street, was totally unfurnished. The office space itself consisted of four bare walls and a telephone which sat in a corner of the carpeted floor. My unopened boxes of books had been stacked in another corner, reaching to the ceiling. A window graced the front exterior wall, affording a view of the street. Next to it was a door allowing access to the outside. Two interior walls each contained a door, one opening into the sanctuary, the other into an adjacent room that would become our church office. The other exterior wall of my corner office was bare. There was little room left for shelves on which to place my modest library. As a potential office, the room was devoid of any office furniture or equipment, save for the lonely telephone in the corner.

Without a desk, I was faced with having to make some temporary accommodation. As an immediate substitute for an office desk, I found a rickety folding table (an old "card" table) at home and elevated its status to that of an official office desk. Searching through the church, I secured two folding chairs from the social hall, one for my use and one for future office visitors. No one seemed to notice that two chairs were missing from around the tables in the social hall. In a closet of the church I found an ancient Underwood manual typewriter, which skipped spaces as I tapped the space bar. It may have had some value as a bona fide antique, but its value as an efficient piece of office equipment was highly doubtful. Nevertheless, I determined that it would have to do. Even with its deficiencies, the ancient typewriter soon became the primary piece of office equipment, vying with the telephone as the most important tool in the pastor's study. Since the weak and aged folding table could not support the weight of the vintage typewriter, I secured an old, used typewriter table from a local secondhand store. With its obvious wear marks and scratches, it seemed a perfect match for the ancient typewriter. With those bare necessities, I maintained a semblance of an office, producing Sunday messages, Sunday school lessons and prayer meeting studies. When research was required during sermon preparation, I rummaged through the stacked boxes containing my books to find the sought-for volume, restacking the cartons as required to keep the office neat. Awkward as it was, I operated in this fashion for over four months, after which I located a small, used, student's desk. Even though it had obviously seen much better days, it was a treasure considering the durability of the rickety card table that it replaced.

A few steps along the walkway from the front door of the church extending toward the street brought me to the large rural mailbox where a steady flow of envelopes and small packages were delivered. Having left a network of friends from the former church, I expected some personal mail. None came. Instead, the mailbox was stuffed with advertisements and an unusual amount of solicitations for donations from various charitable and religious organizations. Occasionally I liberated a trapped cat placed there by young, mischievous neighborhood boys.

The church also received a regular flow of bills notifying us that we were overdue in our payments. After perusing them, I quickly discovered that the church was severely in arrears with its debts and financial obligations. The advertising mail was easily disposed of in the waste basket; so also were the appeals for donations to various radio and television ministries. However, the past-due bills from local businesses and utility companies could not be ignored. Most disturbing of the overdue debts, however, was the monthly demand which we received from a church furniture company in a neighboring state dunning us fifty dollars a month in penalty interest, a result of our delinquency. We owed them for the sanctuary pews, communion table, pulpit, and platform furniture (chairs, modesty shields and choir pews) which had been custom-built for our church. The church was in arrears by several thousand dollars with not a penny paid over the past eighteen months.

Disturbed by this document mailed monthly to the church (evidently an automatic mailing) I placed a call to the church furniture company. Identifying myself to the voice on the other end of the line, I inquired as to the church's debt. The operator connected me with the financial office. A woman's matter-of-fact voice identified herself as the bookkeeper of the company. Identifying myself again, I explained that as the new pastor of the church I intended to lead the congregation into financial solvency, which included paying our past due debts. There was (what I assumed to be) an astonished silence on the other end of the line. I repeated my request to know the full amount which our church owed to their company. After a moment of silence on the line, the feminine voice denied that any record of such a debt existed in their company files. Upon my further insistence that indeed we did owe their company a significant sum, she asked me to wait while she conducted a more thorough search in their files. What I heard next was a most fascinating murmuring on the other end of the line. "No.... No," I heard her murmur as she flipped through files in a cabinet drawer. Then she said, "Sir, I can't seem to find anything that shows that you owe... OH! WHAT'S THIS? There seems to be a file that has dropped down behind the filing drawers. Oh! It's yours! Why, you owe us a great deal of money!" I agreed that we owed their company money for our church furniture and that we wished to begin a payment schedule immediately. She sounded so grateful that it was almost embarrassing. Once the sum was established, she promised that the company would withdraw the penalty interest we had been accumulating. Following the phone call, I dialed my deacon board chairman, a fine, elderly man with many years of experience as a believer. Because he had maintained a common-sense approach to church life, we made an appointment to meet at a local fast-food restaurant.

Henry and I met two days later for breakfast at the local Dairy Queen. There I outlined my "Buy a Pew Campaign" for retiring our financial obligation to the church furniture company. Together we identified all the relevant church furniture and divided the amount owed by the number of pieces which we had ordered. We arrived at a figure and, with our church board's approval, publicized the "Buy a Pew Campaign." The "pew" represented the cost of one unit of furniture, whether an actual pew, chair, or other piece.

At the meeting of the deacons and trustees, Henry and I initially met with some resistance. Several of the men associated with the logging industry protested that they could not afford to "buy" a single pew. I responded by laying Carolyn's and my tax refund for the prior year on the table. "Carolyn and I will buy the first pew," I announced. "How can you afford to do that?" one trustee asked. I responded, "We cannot afford not to! We owe the money, and we can't fail to pay for what we ordered. It's a matter of our testimony for Christ that we pay our debts." Henry immediately responded, "Gladys and I will buy two pews." The Board passed the motion for the "Buy a Pew Campaign" with the board members, committing to help retire the overdue debt by "buying" a pew.

We initially projected that within three months we could retire the entire debt. Unfortunately, we did not reach that goal. One Sunday, however, a lady visitor who was passing through Cottage Grove found her way to our morning service. After the service was over, the ushers received a check from the visitor stipulating that we pay for two pews. Another Sunday an old friend whom we had not seen for over 10 years visited our evening service and donated enough to buy another two pews. And that continued for three more months. Money came from many sources. Finally, at the six-month mark we were able as a church to rejoice in the completion of the campaign. We had paid off the entire debt. With the final check to the church furniture company, I composed a letter of apology expressing deep regret that we had made them wait for so long to receive the just payment which they originally deserved. In return, we received a grateful letter from them commending us for our Christian character and financial integrity. However, we still had other overdue debts to address.

One Sunday morning, during our first three months in the church, prior to the worship service, I asked our custodian not to turn on the heat since we were still in arrears regarding our gas bill. It was cold in the church that Sunday. The members of the congregation did not seem to appreciate my announcement at the offering time. From the pulpit, I addressed the obviously shivering congregation: "We regret that it is so chilly in the sanctuary this morning. However, we are behind in our gas bill. We cannot in good conscience use a product from the gas company which we do not intend to pay for. Therefore, we have not turned up the heat today. We hope that we will soon be able to resume our good relationship with our friends at the gas company." It was clear that we would not be turning on the heat until our past-due heating bills were paid. I feared that my popularity with the congregation would suffer because of this drastic decision on my part. However, following the worship service, an usher excitedly shared with me a note that had been dropped into the offering plate. In terse words it simply said, "Turn on the heat!" Clipped to the note was a twenty-dollar bill. After that Sunday, the people of our church began to give sufficiently to bring our church up-to-date on our overdue bills. It was not necessary for us to resort to that kind of drastic decision again.

Not long after the completion of our "Buy A Pew" campaign, we qualified as a "Mission Aid" church with our Conservative Baptist Church association ministry center and began to be subsidized financially to help us become self-supporting within a three-year period. There is no doubt in my mind that during that time, God provided generously for our church. Beyond that, within the three-year period we did indeed become financially self-supporting. It was the Lord's doing, and it is still marvelous in our eyes.

15

The Sump Pump
January 1970

The first baptism I performed at the Conservative Baptist Church of Cottage Grove was a joyous event -- but its preparation and aftermath created almost insurmountable difficulties.

A twenty-eight-year old lady was the first candidate to be baptized in my new ministry. I looked forward to performing the event with enthusiasm. The baptistry was simply a built-in rectangular cement box at floor level in the slightly raised platform of the church auditorium. Obviously, it was poorly designed, for all that could be seen of a baptism from the front row of the church were the head and shoulders of those in the baptistry itself. Consequently, it was nearly impossible for anyone behind those seated in the first row of the congregation to see anything transpiring down in the baptistry. Concluding that the baptism would be nearly impossible to view, since the pastor and the baptismal candidate stood below floor level, I planned to invite the members of the church to gather on the platform around the water-filled tank to witness the baptism. Although it was a most informal arrangement, it became a tradition which endured over the fifteen years of our ministry in that church. But that tradition was threatened by a perplexity of problems from the very beginning.

Following the morning worship service in my sixth week of pastoral ministry, I gathered the leaders of the church together and asked for instructions on how to fill the baptistry and heat the water for the event scheduled for that evening. Basing my expectations on my limited knowledge of preparing for baptisms, I naively assumed that it would be a simple procedure to fill, heat, and drain a baptistry that held a relatively small amount of water. In the larger churches where I had served in the field of Christian Education, the baptistries were well-designed, carefully plumbed and adequately heated. My expectations were high. Little did I realize how off-the-mark my presuppositions were when it came to preparation for a baptism and the aftermath of draining the baptistry in this small mission church. No thought of the resulting humidity factor in a small church even crossed my mind.

In answer to my question regarding the location of the baptistry system in the small church to which I had recently been called, I was shown two faucets protruding high in the wall of the cement baptistry tank. Next to them was a round hole in the cement wall, serving as an overflow safety feature, designed to drain rising water into a drywell located underneath the church. Unimpressed with the primitive nature of the design, I was further astounded to find the "baptistry heater" to be a small, fifteen-gallon, quick recovery hot water heater, hidden in a small, enclosed cabinet in the men's restroom. Even with my inexperience and my naive expectations, I realized that something was seriously amiss.

Surprised to learn that the actual baptistry capacity in our small church was over five hundred gallons it did not need much calculation to realize that even several hours between the end of the morning service and the beginning of the evening service would not allow us the time necessary to fill the baptistry with heated water. This was confirmed a few minutes later when we turned on the hot water spigot in the baptistry. As the contents of the quick recovery water heater spread along the bottom of the baptistry followed now by the gush of cold water from the same hot water spigot, the board members and I realized that we had an urgent problem. As we turned off the faucet, I stared in dismay at the two inches of cooling water lying in the bottom of the baptistry. Fifteen gallons of hot water was becoming tepid, then cool as the cold cement walls of the baptistry sucked the heat out of the water. Appalled that a Baptist church would not have designed a functioning baptistry, I quickly drafted the trustees of the church to drop all their plans for the afternoon and dedicate themselves to the task of filling the baptistry with warm water.

They rose to the challenge, showing up at the church following their Sunday dinners. But with all the trips from the church kitchen at the rear of the building, across the narthex, through the double doors of the sanctuary and down the center aisle to the baptistry, their pails, coffee pots and sauce pans full of boiling water could not keep up with the cooling effects of the cold cement construction of the baptistry tank. By 5:30 p.m. it became evident that we had lost the battle. Bowing to the inevitable, we turned on the other spigot and filled the remainder of the baptistry with the cold water to make up the volume necessary for immersing an adult body.

That evening, as I entered the waist-high cold water, I silently sympathized with the young lady about to be immersed. Uttering the sacred formula ("Upon profession of your faith, I baptize you in the name of the Father and of the Son and of the Holy Spirit"), I quickly put her down into the icy cold water and pulled her upright before the shock set in. A deaconess greeted her immediately with several bath towels to wrap around the young lady, who was already trembling from the cold. Relieved that the baptism had been successful, if not bone-chilling, I quickly dried off in the men's room, changed back into my Sunday clothes, and returned to the auditorium to continue the rest of the evening service.

Following the conclusion of the service, I realized that standing water in the baptistry might create enough humidity overnight to generate the growth of mould, but I could not locate the drain plug in the floor of the baptistry. Before the church emptied of the Sunday evening participants, I cornered Delbert, one of the leaders of the church who had helped to build the church building. In answer to my question,

"Where is the drain in the baptistry?" his response stunned me, "What drain?" I responded, "All baptistries have drains to release the water following the baptism, but the floor of this baptistry is solid concrete." Rather stupidly I asked again, "Where is the drain?" Blithely he replied, "Oh, that. We didn't know what that hole was for at the time we built it, so we cemented over it." I persisted, "Well, how do you drain the baptistry?" Shrugging his shoulders, he replied simply, "Don't know." Exasperated, I demanded with rising volume, "Well, how did you drain the baptistry the last time you used it?" His answer ended the conversation, "We ain't never used it before."

The next morning I stopped in at the local plumbing store. Like many establishments in a small town, this company stocked a full line of plumbing items. Like many business concerns in small communities, it not only employed a cadre of plumbers but also carried a full inventory of plumbing supplies and equipment. As I explained my predicament to the management, they shook their heads with unbelief. Stifling their mirth, they generously offered me the free use of a large, greasy pump with a ten-foot length of four-inch diameter hose, instructing me on the proper use of the device.

Back at church, I placed the pump on a protective barrier of newspaper so as to avoid staining the carpet of the platform from the grease and dirt which had accumulated on the pump from prior usages. Identifying with local firemen, whom I had seen attaching huge hoses to fire hydrants, I connected the large hose to the pump as per the instructions of the management of the plumbing store and lowered the remaining length of the hose into the water-filled baptistry. A large wire bulb covered the intake of the hose to filter out any foreign objects that might be sucked into the pump. A second length of hose was already attached to the out-feed side of the pump. The end of this hose I draped out the nearest window of the church, which opened directly to the parking area. Carefully I placed the end of the hose beyond the narrow flower bed directly below the window so as not to flush away the tender flowering plants against the building. As I turned on the power switch, the pump roared to life and began to aggressively flush the five hundred gallons of water out the window of the church into the dirt and gravel parking lot. All went as expected for several minutes until the process ceased suddenly as the water level dropped below the wire bulb and the suction broke. Automatically the pump shut itself off, leaving at least five inches of water remaining in the bottom of the baptistry.

Realizing that the water could not remain there throughout the day, I found a pitcher and cup in the church kitchen and spent the rest of the morning scooping up water from the bottom of the baptistry with the cup, pouring it into the pitcher, then climbing the five steps to the level of the platform and on to the nearest window, emptying the pitcher into the flower bed directly below. It took me all morning. The final stage of cleanup was to mop the baptistry floor, wring the mop water into a bucket and repeat the climb up the steps to empty the bucket. I finished just before lunch, convinced that this was not something that my seminary instructors had taught me to anticipate.

The next baptism was scheduled within a few short weeks, again on a Sunday evening. Knowing that we would discourage baptisms unless we could conduct them in water of a comfortable temperature, I again recruited the Trustee Board to provide warm water for the baptistry, resigned that I would have to repeat the emptying process once again. The men of the board assured me and reassured me again that we would have warm water for the event that night. After Sunday dinner, I returned to the church to find a bizarre sight at the baptistry. One of the trustees had rigged a coil of thin copper tubing originating from the faucet inside the baptistry wall out to the platform and back into the baptistry. A large propane "plumber's pot," hissing with an open flame, was heating the coil. True, the water dripping from the copper tube into the baptistry was warm, but the flow was so weak that it would have taken several weeks to fill the baptistry with 500 gallons of water. Meanwhile, fumes from the plumber's pot were filling the auditorium. Other trustees were rushing back and forth from the church kitchen with the usual assortment of vessels filled with small amounts of boiling water. To our dismay, the baptism that evening was again a shockingly cold affair. Following the service, a wheezing older lady in the church accosted me with the statement, "If your baptisms are going to stink like this, I can't come anymore to those services." Apparently, the fumes from the open flame of the "plumber's pot" had overcome the naturally pleasant atmosphere within the sanctuary.

The next morning the plumbing establishment lent me their sump pump with sympathy, hiding the mirth behind their eyes. Again, our parking lot became a sea of mud.

As we planned the third baptism, scheduled for a few weeks later, one of the trustees of the church assured me that he would have sixty gallons of boiling hot water for the baptistry by 5:30 that evening, in time for the 6:00 p.m. event. We agreed that we could fill the remainder, necessary for a baptism with cold water, resulting in a comfortably warm baptismal environment. His plan was ingenious. Leaving church that morning, he went directly downtown and purchased two thirty-gallon plastic garbage cans. Following his Sunday dinner, he managed to empty the contents of the two thirty-gallon water heaters in his garage into the garbage cans situated in the back of his pickup truck. Carefully, he negotiated the irregularities of the four-mile dirt road from his house to the edge of town, turned slowly onto the paved highway, and gently drove to the church. Feeling buoyed by the success of his plan, he turned a little too sharply into the church's dirt parking lot, abruptly dumping sixty gallons of boiling water into the bed of his truck as the two garbage cans tipped over from the force of his turn.

I heard what sounded like profanity, which suddenly stopped as I approached him in my Sunday suit. In answer to my question, "Where is the water?" he answered, "Here," as he opened the tailgate. Sixty gallons of hot water gushed onto the surface of the dirt parking lot. At that point, all my frustration at our ice-cold baptism services boiled over. "Listen," I threatened as I poked my finger at his chest for emphasis, "we had better have 60 gallons of hot water here within the next half hour or there will be a disaster in the making!" Inwardly, I imagined the Deacon Board summoning me before them to give an account of my ineptness and failure to be able to complete as simple a task as a baptism.

It only took a phone call to the Deacon Board Chairman, Tom Douglas, to discover that he had two thirty-gallon water heaters. It was a short trip to drive the three blocks to his house and reload the garbage cans once again. Driving back to the church over paved streets was much simpler than compensating for travel over rough, unpaved roads. To insure against another calamity, I sat on the fender-well in the back of the pickup and steadied the two steaming garbage cans. One can only imagine what the onlookers on the streets must have thought as they saw the Baptist pastor sitting in the back of a pickup truck, steadying two steaming cans of water in his Sunday finery.

Although it was not an easy task to empty two garbage cans of hot water, we managed to do it the old -fashioned way, rushing from the truck through the church to the baptistry. We finished just in time for the service to begin. By that time, I was almost exhausted and perspiring profusely from the effort. Nevertheless, the baptism service proceeded without any hint of what it took to prepare for it. Although the water was cool, it was not uncomfortably so. Again, the next morning, I was reduced to emptying the baptistry as I had done before.

After this incident, I convened the Trustee Board in a special session to address the dilemma. Presenting the problem, I explained that I would not be conducting baptisms in freezing water as I had been doing and waited for their response. The Trustee Board was made up of loggers and blue-collar workers. Several theories were advanced to solve the problem, but limited finances sank each proposal. Finally, one trustee suggested that we have a special work day and tunnel under the church to place a giant hot plate underneath the baptistry to heat the cement floor, hoping that this would effectively heat the water. He was serious. I asked as patiently as I could, "And where would we get a giant hot plate?" "I don't know," came the reply. "There's got to be one somewhere." The others agreed, nodding solemnly. "Supposing that there is a giant hotplate somewhere for purchase," I asked as patiently as I could, "how could we afford the electricity required to operate it?"

The members of the trustee board sheepishly shrugged their shoulders in silent defeat. Trying to keep the mounting sarcasm which I felt out of my voice, I managed to calmly disagree with them and suggest that we procure a submersible baptistry heater, a "tea warmer" type which was commercially available. Unfortunately, those baptistry heaters were prohibitively expensive for our struggling church. The meeting ended without a solution to the problem. However, I urged them to pray with me for an answer to our needs.

It was not long in coming. A family which had moved from Eastern Oregon to Cottage Grove visited our church and shortly thereafter joined the fellowship. Ken Willis was an electrical engineer whose experience included designing mini-circuits for space satellites. When he became aware of our problem, he volunteered to design a baptistry heater for our church. He even built it at his own expense. Thus our third baptism was a physically comfortable experience for all concerned.

Still, I faced the problem of emptying the baptistry. The men of the church could not help since they were all employed during the day, so after the third baptism I decided not to use our baptistry again. This would mean that we must ask some neighboring church if we could share theirs. I was unhappy with this alternative.

My ministerial colleagues in the Emerald Association of the Conservative Baptists shook their heads in sympathy after they had finished laughing as I told them of my frustration. A solution seemed to elude us...until one day not too long after, when I received a phone call from a person whom I did not know. He was calling from Albany, Oregon, many miles north of our church. He was laughing as he asked, "Is this Pastor Kooshian?" When I verified his assumption, he chuckled again and said, "I heard that story about your baptistry. That's the funniest story

I've heard in a long time." He laughed again. Courteously, I chuckled with him. Inside, I was asking, *"What kind of a kook calls up to laugh at my predicament?"* I was immediately shamed as he said, "I've got a sweet little submersible sump pump here that's brand new. It ought to solve your problem. Just drop it into your baptistry, hook the hose to the overflow right near your water intake (the faucets) and plug her in. The cord is heavy duty and waterproof. You should have no problem." When I asked the cost, he said, "It's a gift to the Lord. We'll drop it off next week."

At our next baptism, we plugged in the baptistry heater and enjoyed the comfort of warm water as we baptized several candidates for church membership. The Trustees had cut a hole in the floor of the baptistry and cemented in a five gallon can upside down. With the bottom of the can removed, it was an ideal fit for the sump pump. All the water in the baptistry was easily sucked out into the overflow well. The plug in the top of the can could be removed for the remaining water to drain into the drywell beneath the baptistry. The cap was then screwed in from what had originally been the inside of the can to keep the water table from flooding the baptistry when it was not in use. With the plug tightly screwed in the can, the baptistry was as waterproof as before.

God had answered our prayers without any expense to the church.

16

Christmas Watch
(Moving Ahead of God)
December 1972

In spite of the Lord's provision, our mentality of deprivation still clung to us as a family. Having to operate too close to the budget for so long was taking its toll. Our "Mission-Aid" church was not yet self-supporting. In practical terms, it meant that in those early months of our ministry in Cottage Grove, we were not getting paid a living wage. With our family of three small children we felt the constant drag of economic pressure upon our outlook upon life. Much of our free time was spent in poring over newspaper advertisements looking for "specials" in grocery and department stores. "Luxury" items such as table lamps, watches, cameras, film, and much needed furniture were well beyond our reach.

But the Lord proved to be faithful in our neediness. Several churches had reached out to us, one neighboring church pledging a monthly support of fifty dollars. A women's missionary society from a large church in Salem, Oregon, sporadically sent us boxes of used clothes, some of which were not appropriate for our children to wear due to condition, style or fit. While some garments were repairable, others were too stained to be worn.

Two other nearby churches sponsored a few "showers" of food and clothing to help us through the thin times. However, the subtle financial pressures upon our family took their toll upon our faith in ever achieving financial security. Yet, in spite of all our fears due to the constant economic pressure, we did not miss a meal or forego any payments on rent or utilities. Still, we felt that we could not indulge our impulses to purchase items or attend events which our neighbors and friends took almost for granted. Concerts, plays, and movies were beyond our reach. A lengthy part of our children's growing years went unrecorded because we could not afford a camera. Without our awareness, our sense of privation imprisoned our thinking.

So in November of our first year at the church, when a sale of Timex watches was advertised in the local papers, we set our hearts upon purchasing a fifteen dollar watch for Carolyn, whose own watch had stopped working several weeks before.

We could not simply rush out and make the purchase, for in our financial extremity, a transaction of this magnitude required some careful examination. The cost seemed exorbitant for us to simply splurge on our desires. In deep discussion together, we weighed the pros and cons of such an extravagance. After all, God had been providing for all our needs. Why could we not trust Him for a watch? We could make known our needs in prayer to Him, and if He felt that it was a necessity, would He not provide it? We desired to trust in God. Still, the allure of that new watch "on sale" was as powerful to us as a truly expensive piece of jewelry.

Finally, we decided that we could not afford to wait, though none of our generous supporters knew that Carolyn needed a watch. If we delayed beyond the expiration date of the sale printed in the advertisement, it would be too late. We put behind us the realization that we were violating our own budget even if we justified the purchase as taking advantage of a money-saving sale price. I rationalized the thought of purchasing the watch by asking myself, *"What really are the chances that a supporting church would notice that Carolyn needed a watch?"*

Not feeling totally convinced, but mutually supporting one another, we decided to spend part of our precious limited resources on that watch, and before long we were admiring the beauty of it on Carolyn's wrist.

A couple of weeks later we received a phone call from a lady representing the women's missionary circle of her church. She told us that she had been selected to deliver a box of Christmas gifts for us and for our children on behalf of their society. Their church had adopted us as their "Christmas Project." As before, we were excited at the prospect of her visit.

On the appointed day, she showed up at our door with a box loaded with gaily wrapped boxes for our children. As she lifted the gifts out of the box one by one, she examined them to make sure that the correct identification appeared on each gift.

After all the gifts were piled upon our sofa beside her, the lady beamed and pulled a small box out of her purse. She said with joy, "And this is for Carolyn. We noticed that she did not have a watch on her wrist the last time we saw her, and we wanted to give her this one to be opened before Christmas." A sense of dread came over me as Carolyn unwrapped the decorative paper from the box. Opening it, she discovered the exact same watch we had purchased a short time before. In the next breath, I breathed a sigh of relief that Carolyn had not worn her new watch that day!

However, we had admittedly stepped ahead of God's provision! While we thanked our guest profusely for all the gifts, and especially the beautiful watch, I was acutely aware that we had spent money which we did not need to sacrifice simply because we were in too much of a hurry to allow God to meet our needs.

Nothing drastic happened as the result of our decision, but we were acutely aware of missing out on the joy of having God provide for our needs. Rather than waiting on a faithful and gracious God, we had rushed ahead of Him in trying to provide for our needs on our own.

We missed the joy of realizing that even for our desire of a cheap watch we could have trusted God to meet our need.

17

Insurance Money
March 1974

It was Friday afternoon, and the financial situation in our home was bordering on desperate. We needed $75 to meet an imminent insurance payment, due on Monday only three days away. To complicate the problem, we had inadequate assets with which to meet the upcoming bill. All that remained of our finances was a mere $25.00, not one penny more, not one penny less. Little did we suspect at that time the significance of that circumstance; later it would become clear.

All our assets had been exhausted in the interim period between leaving our last church and coming to the small mission church where we served. We had come to a church that was on the verge of financial collapse, hoping that we could make a difference in its growth. But soon we discovered that they could not really support a pastor and his family. Consequently, money in our household was scarce. However, all our mathematical manipulations could not stretch the $25 in our possession to meet our upcoming obligation.

The immediate challenge facing us was that I was scheduled to speak at the Berean Baptist Church's high school weekend conference at SeaCrest Lodge in Newport, Oregon. After checking a map, I discovered that the trip was two hundred miles, each way. Ordinarily that would not be a problem. But the needle hovered on "empty" in the fuel gauge of our old Volkswagen Square Back. And it was time for me to leave for the conference. Carolyn was to stay home and care for our three small children.

She solemnly handed me the $25, reminding me that this was all we had, with no payday immediately in sight.

So we prayed together and committed our situation to God. I kissed my wife farewell as she prompted me to remember the stop at the gas station. She did not want me to stall on the road somewhere out of gas. Bidding her farewell, I mentioned that I should be home late Sunday afternoon. At a nearby gas station I topped off the tank, hoping that a tankful of gasoline would be enough to get me to the conference and back home without having to stop for an additional refill. The gasoline cost $17.53. Resisting the urge to purchase a snack, I pocketed the change and hurried on toward my destination.

Soon I forgot my financial anxieties regarding our dwindling resources as my mind focused upon the conference ahead. I was eagerly looking forward to the experience of sharing the Lord with high school young people. Berean Baptist Church in Eugene, Oregon had an energetic youth ministry under the competent and enthusiastic leadership of Lamar Allen. I looked forward to spending time with this particular youth pastor and his exciting group of counsellors and teenagers. My friendship with the pastor of the church and with Lamar was one of long standing. It was their church which was helping to financially support our family and our ministry in Cottage Grove.

Upon arrival, after a two-hour drive, I discovered SeaCrest Lodge in a most beautiful natural setting. Sandwiched between the Coast Highway and the sands of Agate Beach, SeaCrest Lodge with its tall pine trees gave an initial impression of being in the timber-laden mountains of central Oregon, an impression quickly erased by the sound of the pounding surf against the rocks at the bottom of a small cliff descending to sea level. A brown carpet of pine needles muffled the sound of those who wandered about, admiring the beauty of the surroundings.

When I stepped from my car, I was warmly greeted by the Lamar and his staff of counsellors. The youth counsellors and I had known each other from various activities of our Conservative Baptist fellowship in years past and had long ago cemented our bonds of friendship.

The rapport between me and the high school youth of Berean Baptist Church was easily established, for my twin brother had served in the youth ministry of their church a few years earlier, and many of the youth still remembered him. Some of the young people knew me from the times I had been invited to be a guest speaker in the pulpit of their church. Their warmth paved the way for easy acceptance with those others whom I did not know.

The weekend went quickly as I entered the activities of the youth and became one with them. I had prepared individual booklets for the conference, which served as study guides for the youth. They seemed to manifest an enthusiasm for the study of Growing in Christ, based upon the printed materials of Campus Crusade for Christ, so it became a rich spiritual experience for us all. Bible study times interspersed with fun activities, sport events, great food, and exploration of the beach, searching for agates, combined to build a sense of close camaraderie among us all.

The weekend passed all too soon. Filled with spiritually nurturing experiences and joyful memories, the conference ended after noon lunch on Sunday.

A different spirit descended over the conference as campers packed hurriedly. preparing for the bus ride back to their church, where anxious parents awaited. While I regretted the end of such a positive and enjoyable weekend, I was also eager to return to my beloved wife and family.

As I packed my sleeping bag and the few clothes which I had brought with me, Lamar approached, offering me an envelope containing a fifty-dollar check. It was the honorarium to cover my travel expenses. I was grateful.

The packing for the trip home now completed, I paused and took one final nostalgic look at the camp and the youth scurrying toward their church bus. Heading for my car, I gave thanks to God for the wonderful weekend and the for blessings I had received as camp pastor.

Suddenly a voice hailed me by name. As I turned, I saw Lamar Allen hurrying toward me. Speaking slightly breathlessly, he said, "The kids so appreciated your ministry this weekend that they took a special love offering to be added to the honorarium. It isn't much, but it is an expression of their gratitude and love." Into my hands he placed an envelope heavy with coins and a few bills. Bidding me goodbye, he hurried away toward the church bus awaiting him.

Wonderingly, I stared at the envelope as the bus pulled away from the Lodge. When I looked up, I found myself alone beside my car. The enthusiastic commotion typical of high school youth was now simply a fresh memory.

The church bus carrying the campers home exited the campground, turning onto a small road leading to the Coast Highway. Alone in the quietness, I could hear the distinct sound of the surf accompanying the rustling of the wind through the towering pines. Eager to see what had been placed in my hands, I opened the envelope and counted the love offering.

It totaled an odd sum of $19.53. Something clicked in my mind, so I did some quick calculations. God was sending me a message. In my possession I now had the following:

$50.00 Conference Honorarium
$19.53 Love Offering
$ 7.47 left over from purchasing gasoline

The total was $77.00, enough to meet our insurance premium. Checking the gas gauge of the car, I noticed that it was not yet half empty so I would have plenty of gas for the trip home and enough left over to buy a snack on the way. This was surely a fulfillment of the "exceeding abundantly above all that we can ask or think" promise. God had again proved His faithfulness!

18

Money from The Mud
August 1977

The church social at the home of one of our church member families was located high on a hillside in the Southern Oregon Mountains, just south of Cottage Grove. The constantly falling rain in the fading evening twilight did not make the trip as pleasant as it would have been in fair weather. But after all, this was Oregon, and the beautiful green of our out-of-doors came at the price of abundant rain. A winding dirt road ascended the hillside to the house, which had been built reminiscent of the Swiss chalets of the owners' home country. Without the paving of the road or the orderly lines of curbs on each side, the trip uphill required concentration. In the dark, the return trip downhill could possibly be hazardous.

That did not keep the members of the church from attending. As we drove to the imposing house, we saw several cars parked in the adjoining meadow. Stepping out of the car, Carolyn and I walked gingerly through the wild wet grass to a wet path leading to the makeshift steps at the front door. Stepping on a slab of wood which served as a step, I assisted Carolyn into the house. Because of the muddy ground that clung to the bottom of our shoes, we were required to remove our shoes immediately before moving from the entryway to the interior of the house.

At the party was a couple with their two young boys. The father of the family worked in the woods as a tree thinner. His job was to cut down undesirable saplings to make room for the other, more viable trees to grow. It was demanding work, for the tree thinner had to carry at least two chain saws as he climbed up steep slopes to thin trees for a potentially larger harvest later. But with the downturn in the logging industry, he was currently without employment. Finances for his family were thin, and expenses continued at their normal rate.

When we learned of their need, Carolyn and I quietly determined between ourselves to give a fifty-dollar anonymous gift to them through a mutual friend in the church. We did not have the money at that time, but we were hoping and praying that the Lord would provide, though we did not know how He could possibly bring that amount of money into our possession. The party was an enjoyable affair as church members visited with each other over light refreshments. It was dark when the party ended. The rain had stopped, and we all left while it was convenient to do so.

As we stepped out the door at the end of the party, I happened to glance down at the large slice of log that served as a temporary step. Its cover of mud did not hide the fact that it was a huge slice of curly maple with all its intricate patterns and inherent coloring. I asked my host, "If I buy you some paver stones to make a step here, would you let me have this piece of wood?" He replied, "Take it! I have other pieces of wood I can put in its place." He lifted the large slice of wood out of the mud, hosed it off and handed the wet wood to me. Wrapping it in old newspapers, we placed it in the trunk of the car and drove home.

It took a week for the wood slice to dry out. Fortunately, the moisture in the ground had not permeated deeply into the dense hardwood. As I sanded it smooth in my garage, the beauty of the wood fairly leaped out at me. It was a magnificent multicolored cross section of the trunk of a maple burl. After drilling a hole in the center of the wood, I routed out a large rectangle into the back of the piece. It was time for the final sanding.

On a warm day, while I was giving the piece its finish sanding, one of my neighbors happened by. After asking me what I was working on, I showed her the sanded surface, a beautiful combination of natural color and design. "A clock," I responded. "It is just ready for a finishing coat and the installation of a clock-work." Eagerly she asked, "Is it for sale?" I had been thinking of hanging the beautiful finished clock in our house, but inspiration struck me. "I might be willing to sell it." She immediately asked, "How much?" Impulsively, I responded, "Fifty dollars." Immediately she exclaimed "Sold!" She had thought that it would be at least three times that amount.

Within a week, the clock was finished. As the fifty-dollar bill was placed in an envelope, we thanked the Lord for His provision and quickly forwarded the money to our mutual friend, who delivered it to the needy family. Not only did they rejoice at the anonymous gift, but we rejoiced in the creative way the Lord had provided money from the mud.

19

The Chevy Impala
April 1977

"Our car is dying." Carolyn looked up from the book she was reading and received my stark statement with a glance of concern. I continued, "We need a newer car. The maintenance costs on this car are draining our finances. We can't afford to fix one problem, only to have something else break or wear out." Carolyn responded, "We cannot afford a new car now. We can barely afford another used one." The silence hung over us as we grappled with the thought of having to pay for a replacement vehicle.

The problem was starkly apparent. While our current vehicle was failing, our young family was growing. What had been an adequate means of transportation when purchased five years earlier was one no longer. Our family of three small children had grown, but the passenger space in our small foreign car had not. The mechanical failures were increasing in frequency. Our budget could not support the constant cost of maintaining an older vehicle, yet the necessity of reliable mobility was urgent.

It did not take much calculation for us to realize that we were racing rapidly toward a financial crisis. The effectiveness of our ministry depended, in part, on reliable transportation. Visiting church members, calling upon the sick and driving daily to various appointments demanded problem-free mobility. Further, the occasional yearly conferences, college board meetings and annual national gatherings often required long distance travel. There was no doubt in our minds that it was time to purchase a more reliable means of transportation. However, we were acutely aware that our finances were limited.

After having exhaustively investigated several "pre-owned" (used) and new car possibilities, we came up empty-handed. The available choices somehow did not fit our needs. Size of the automobile, cost, condition, mileage and age all were factors that had to be taken into consideration.

In desperation, I called our ministry center (church headquarters) and inquired of Dr. Charles Losie, our General Director, as to whether he knew of any car dealers who would consider a clergy discount. "Look," I explained, "we need to purchase a car, preferably a used one. Do you know of anyone in the automobile business who can help us?" Dr. Losie was sympathetic. As an experienced pastor himself, he understood our predicament. "I think I know just the person you need to see, the sales manager at Weiler Chevrolet in Oregon City. His name is Earl Metz. I am sure that he can help you. Just use my name. Tell him that I recommended him to you." Just before he ended the call, he gave me directions to the dealership about 80 miles north of our home in Cottage Grove.

Picking up the phone, I dialed the Weiler dealership and was connected by the operator with Mr. Earl Metz. "Hello, this is Earl Metz." The voice was strong and confident. After I explained my reason for calling, mentioning that Dr. Losie had recommended him to me, he said, "I am sure that we can work out something that will meet your needs. Why don't you come on up and see what we can do for you? Perhaps we can get you into a new car." I hesitated, fearful that I would be manipulated into buying a new vehicle which Carolyn and I could ill-afford. "We really cannot afford a new car," I replied. "We are looking forward to a more modest purchase." At my hesitation, I heard him chuckle on the other end of the line. "Why don't you come up; we'll see if there is any possibility of getting you into a new car. I am sure we can find something that you can afford. After all, I could offer you a really good deal." My heart fell as the thought gripped me that this might just be another manipulation by an over-eager car salesman.

Afterward, while reviewing the phone call with my wife, I rehearsed the reasons why we could not afford a new automobile. "New cars cost too much." "We don't have the income to support payments." "What will our church members think if they were to see the pastor and family driving up to church in a brand-new car?

Apparently, the wearying search for an automobile had taken its toll on my confidence. At the car dealership where we had first begun our search, the salesman had dismissed Carolyn and me by saying, "If you can't commit now to buying a car from us, we can't be bothered to waste time showing you automotive vehicles." Somehow, we felt that the salesman lacked subtlety in automotive salesmanship. I thought at the time, *"How did it make sense to commit to buying an automobile before knowing what was available and whether we could afford it?"* We thanked him and politely excused ourselves from the showroom.

At another dealership, the salesman employed a sales tactic designed to impress the buyer. Walking toward the sales office, the agency representative remarked, "Let me check with my manager to see if he would approve of selling you a car at a discount." It was a line we had heard at other dealerships. I wondered as he walked away, *"Do all the salesmen from these different car dealers we have visited attended the same salesmanship school?"* Years later I discovered that, in fact, the tactic was widespread and most certainly bogus. These salesmen did not have to "check" with their managers. It was simply a delaying maneuver to "hook" the customer into thinking that the price was being reduced when it was simply a part of the negotiation. The real price was far below the one listed on the driver's side window of the vehicle. No real discount was being offered.

Several days later, as I drove north toward my destination in Oregon City, my sales resistance continued to rise. *"Could this simply be a waste of time and effort? Was this salesman going to be just like the rest?"* Doubts and questions plagued my mind.

As I drove into the dealership and parked my worn car, I surveyed rows of shiny Chevrolets of different models and sizes, gleaming in the sunshine, their colorful exteriors beckoning me to take a closer look. Parking in a designated space, I became acutely conscious of the contrast between my old car and the new models all around. Resolutely, I closed my mind to their enticement and walked through the open double-doors into the showroom. Immediately I was approached by a salesman. "Can I help you?" he asked in greeting. "Yes. Is Mr. Earl Metz here?" I responded. "I have an appointment with him." The salesman answered. Just a moment, I'll let him know that you are here."

A few moments later a tall, rather well-built man approached me, a broad smile on his face. "I'm Earl Metz." He strode forward, hand extended. "Are you Pastor Kooshian?" "Yes," I stammered. "I wondered if you have a reliable used automobile. I can't afford much, but I do need dependable transportation." The words seemed to spill out of my mouth as if they had been memorized. He countered, "Have you considered a new car?" "No," I admitted, adding, "We simply can't afford it."

He put his arm around my shoulders as he led me to his office. "Hey," he whispered confidentially, "We Christians need to stick together. Let me see what I can do for you."

I was surprised at the warmth and camaraderie that this man demonstrated. He acted as if I was a member of his family. It was true, of course in a spiritual sense, for we were equal members of the Family of God.

However, my own sense of financial inadequacy gripped me as I remonstrated, "We really can't afford a new car." I thought to myself,

"Have I made a mistake in coming this distance for an appointment with a man whom I have never met? Is he just another slick car salesman? Earl Metz paused, stopping our forward motion. It was as if he had read my mind. "Look," he said, "we're talking wholesale here. I can make you a deal that you can afford. Come on into my office and let's see what we can do."

As the next minutes unfolded, my confidence grew. Earl Metz presented me with the idea of purchasing a new 1977 nine-passenger Chevy Impala station wagon with many convenient accessories. As I demurred at each suggestion of an expensive accessory package, Earl Metz reminded me, "Remember, its wholesale." He guided me through the purchasing procedure until we finally arrived at an affordable price for the car. Still, I hesitated. Seeming to understand my reluctance, Earl patted me on the shoulder and suggested, "Why don't you go home and talk it over with your wife and pray about it? You can call me with your decision. The offer will still be available."

Driving home, I did not realize the extent to which Carolyn's and my sense of penury had affected our outlook on life. At home, I reviewed the experience with my wife, telling her about the remarkable salesman who was bending over backwards to see that we could afford a new car. Speaking with her about our family, I betrayed my confidence in the promise of God to meet our needs. "We're not fancy enough to drive around in a shiny new red station wagon," I reasoned. I could not wrap my mind around the idea of driving a large new car.

As we reviewed our meager savings, we discovered that spread out over three years, the payments presented a financial challenge. We would have to be sure that this was the will of the Lord. Carolyn was initially as reluctant as I. Yet, as we prayed over the decision, we began to come to a biblical conclusion. We remembered that the Lord was leading the Children of Israel into the Promised Land but that the nation refused to follow the Lord's leading. As a result, they wandered in the wilderness for forty years as the disobedient generation died and their children grew to gain the conquest of the Promised Land.

Questions grew in our minds. *"Was God offering us the "Promised Land" in the purchase of a new car at a deep discount? Were we on the verge of disobedience if we turned down the only respectable offer we had encountered in our automobile search?"* As we prayed and considered the offer, the more we became confident that God was providing us a grand alternative to the other poor options before us.

Two weeks later, the decision was made. Before long we made the trip to Oregon City, this time returning with a magnificent, shiny new 1977 Chevrolet Impala station wagon.

As if to place a definite exclamation point on our purchase, the Lord sent us a message through an unlikely source a few days later. The phone call was from one of the automobile dealers whose business we had visited several weeks earlier and had rejected the deal that was offered. Identifying himself, he asked, "Have you found a car yet?" "Yes," I answered. "We found such a good deal we could not turn it down."

The voice on the other end of the phone sounded disappointed. After a moment of silence, he inquired, "May I ask what automobile you bought?" Before answering him, I thought to myself, *"What harm is there in being open with the details of my purchase, so long as I do not identify the firm or individual from whom I purchased the new vehicle?"* Drawing a breath, I answered, "A 1977 Chevy Impala station wagon."

"Do you mind my asking how much you paid for it?" he persisted. "No, I don't mind at all." I kept my voice flat and neutral. "We paid five thousand, five hundred dollars," I said after a pause. For a moment there was silence on the other end of the line. Then with some unbelief in his voice the dealer said, "That's an incredible deal! If you are telling me the truth, that dealer did not make any money at all on that car. In fact, he probably took a loss." I answered, "I am being totally honest. That is what we paid for the car." Slowly, the voice on the other end of the phone line said, "I couldn't beat that price. You really received a great deal!" After that conclusion, he thanked me and hung up the phone.

The 1977 Chevrolet Impala station wagon was indeed God's car. That same year I suffered severe injuries in an automobile accident as a passenger in my brother's small sports car. He and I picked up his son from work and were driving toward home when we were struck by a larger vehicle almost head-on. The driver of the other vehicle was heavily impaired by alcohol. Each of us was hospitalized with serious injuries, and after corrective surgery, I spent three weeks in a hospital in Livermore, California.

When I was well enough to be transported to Oregon, Carolyn was notified that the medical transportation for her husband would have to be by helicopter, costing thousands of dollars, not covered by insurance. It was a sum which we could not afford. As we talked it over that night, I suggested, "Carolyn, do you suppose that if we put a mattress in the back of the station wagon, that perhaps my physician would be amenable to that alternative mode of transportation? After all, the car does have air conditioning. The suspension is new. With proper bedding and pillows, I could sleep comfortably on the way to the Cottage Grove Hospital." Carolyn was enthusiastic. "The children have already been taken to Roy's home in Ashland, Oregon. Roy could come down and help me drive you to his house. We could get a couple of men from our church to drive down to Ashland and take us the rest of the way to Cottage Grove."

When Carolyn relayed that alternative mode of transportation, the physician in charge of my care wholeheartedly agreed. The day was very warm when we departed from the Livermore hospital, but our new station wagon negotiated the heat of the day and the stress of uphill driving with ease. Lying in the back, I was as comfortable as in my hospital bed. The trip was made with comparatively little expense.

As our children grew, we still had room for them in our car. The extra room in the nine-passenger station wagon even allowed us to transport furniture that would have otherwise required delivery costs.

The station wagon was paid off in three years, and with very little cost in maintenance, we drove it for many more years. During the duration of our children's college years, we did not have the additional burden of car payments, freeing us to address college expenses. When we eventually moved to a new ministry in a different city, we used our station wagon to transport the church youth to various activities and events.

After nineteen years, we sold the station wagon to friends at a nominal cost. It was still a very reliable and dependable vehicle. Without a doubt, the 1977 Impala station wagon was the Lord's incredible provision for us throughout a changing time in our lives, a time when we needed a vehicle that would not incur repair costs while our children were in college.

We found new meaning to the promise of God in Psalm 34:10, "The young lions do lack, and suffer hunger: but they that seek the LORD shall not want any good thing."

20

Downpayment
August 1978

Seven years had passed in our first pastoral ministry in Cottage Grove. Our children had grown. Suzanne was a fourteen-year-old teenager trying to exercise all the rights of a firstborn child, challenged by an eleven-year-old sister and a nine-and-a-half-year-old younger brother who seemed to annoy her constantly. So Carolyn and I found ourselves focused upon rearing an active family in the "nurture and admonition of the Lord." One of the limitations we faced was the constantly shrinking living space in our small half of a duplex. The two-bedroom, single bath half of the duplex which we occupied offered adequate room for our children, but as they grew, we found that even with the bonus room, space became tighter and tighter for our maturing family. Moving Suzanne down to the second bedroom only relieved the problem temporarily.

Finances were still tight. Even though the church had achieved self-support within the three-year condition of our mission aid, our meager salary did not improve significantly. The outstanding church debts that had piled up into a formidable financial challenge upon our arrival had been finally paid, so all that remained of a financial encumbrance was the church mortgage. Although the pastoral salary was not by any calculation magnanimous, we still managed through extreme frugality to make ends meet. However, we were not able to save for the future. Beside the day-to-day economic pressures, I became increasingly aware that we were economically locked into being renters. We were not even in the process of purchasing a home. We simply could not afford it.

So it was a surprise when I awoke on New Year's day of 1977 with the strong conviction that we would not be living in our present accommodations by the end of the year. The conviction did not spring from a growing dissatisfaction with our rental duplex but rather with a suddenness that was a complete surprise to me. We had no money with which to make payments on a house. Nor did we have any funds or savings accounts from which to draw money for a downpayment. Even though we were very careful with our money, we still lived from week to week. Yet the strong feeling persisted. I tried to identify myself with Abraham, who was called out of Ur of the Chaldees to a destination known only to God. But there the comparison ended. I could not identify the basis for this new conviction except that it was strong and not something which I had personally generated through dissatisfaction with our current circumstances. Casually I announced to my wife that afternoon, "Somehow, I feel that we will not be living in this place by the end of the year. I don't think that we will be leaving the church, but I do feel strongly for some reason that we will not be living here."

Since I had not conjured up the feeling within myself, I could only conclude that it was a conviction from the Lord. But it was vague and undefined; no details were involved. I muttered to myself, *"At least God spoke audibly to Abraham."*

However, without our knowing it, the Lord was putting the pieces into place for a rather dramatic accomplishment of His will. How could we know that the aged Ukrainian couple who had recently joined our church would be part of God's plan? Mr. and Mrs. Sam Seleshanko were warm "old country" people. Sam was as tall and erect as his wife was small and petite. They were not well off either in riches or in health. The trauma of having lived in a turbulent part of the world, as well as the ravages of old age, had resulted in a slight stooped posture for Mr. Seleshanko. His deep bass voice quavered with age. But this did not keep him from the love of singing. In contrast to his shy and retiring nature, his wife sparkled with warmth. It was evident that she was the social one of the pair. But her fragile health limited her activity in the church. Age had written wrinkles in both of their faces. Both were devout followers of the Lord and loved the fellowship of the church. Because of their very modest means, they carefully nurtured their limited resources, yet gave faithfully to the Lord through the church.

They were the least likely people to serve as instruments in the Lord's plan for our family. Nor did we have any reason to connect my newfound conviction with this rather unassuming aged couple. Whenever their grown children came to visit them, the Seleshankos brought their extended family to church.

Their son, Dan, a realtor, often came to visit his parents and brought his wife and young children with him to church services whenever possible. On his first visit, his parents introduced him to Carolyn and me, proudly announcing that Dan was a successful realtor who lived in Eugene, about twenty-five miles north of Cottage Grove. In the progression of the conversation, I admitted in an attempt at wry humor, "Well, we won't be needing your services. We have barely enough money to rent a single-family home."

Dan Seleshanko quickly disagreed. "You would be surprised how many homes are available at affordable prices. You might be able to buy a house under one of the governmental subsidy programs designed to help people in your economic situation. There are several government programs that enable people to get into a house of their own. In fact, I would be glad to meet with you and show you that it is possible to own a house even with your limited income." Reasoning that his offer was simply the enthusiasm of an aggressive realtor I did not take him seriously. "Thank you," I responded. "But we really are not in the market for a house. We simply cannot afford it." Expecting that my refusal would end the conversation, I was surprised when he countered, "Just let me show you what is available. Then, if you still feel that you are not interested, you can just say so, and that will end the matter." "But," he added, "you just might be surprised."

Carolyn and I glanced at each other, recognizing a flicker of hope in each other's expression. She waited for me to speak. Surrendering to the opportunity, I gave her a slight nod, turned to Dan Seleshanko and said, "Okay, we are willing to see what is available. We don't know much about real estate purchases, but we are willing to hear what you have to say." My statement was more out of curiosity than hope, not really expecting anything serious to come out of such a meeting. I viewed his offer with the same reluctant enthusiasm with which I would greet a door-to-door insurance salesman.

A few days later we met with Dan. As Carolyn and I drove to his office in Eugene, we fortified ourselves with predetermined sales resistance, reasoning together that there really is no such thing as a "free lunch."

Warmly welcoming us, Dan graciously seated us and launched enthusiastically into his presentation. But it was not about the purchase of a house. "Let me show you a little-known governmental program that might change your thinking about a purchase of a house. The Farmers Home Administration (FmHA) Low Income Loan Program is designed to get low-income families into a home of their own. With a small down payment, you can secure a home. The FmHA will then reduce the interest on the loan. In other words, they will pay a significant part of the interest each month, leaving you to pay the principal and a small part of the interest. With that kind of arrangement, house payments could be in reach of your budget. How does that sound?"

We were stunned. We had never heard of such a thing. The government agency would pay a significant part of our monthly payment. It sounded too good to be true. FmHA acquired small, basic houses and sold them to qualified buyers with a very small down- payment. Further, the FmHA subsidized their own loans by reducing the interest rate, allowing the buyer to pay a smaller monthly mortgage payment. A further advantage of the program was that most of the payment each month went to reduce the principal of the loan rather than being almost wholly dedicated to the interest, as was usually true of home mortgages. But there was a warning.

Dan continued, "The application paperwork alone is formidable. It takes from two to six months to complete. You will have to undergo an interview following the acceptance of your paperwork. If you can convince the interviewer that, indeed, your income is as low as your paperwork indicates, that you have no hidden resources, that you are responsible people, and that your debts are not significant, then you might qualify for an FmHa loan." He concluded, "Of course, all of this is contingent upon a house becoming available in your vicinity. At present, the only available homes are here in Eugene. Nothing is available at this time in Cottage Grove or in the greater South Lane County. Are you still interested is applying for this program? Application alone is an arduous process." He paused, awaiting an answer.

Carolyn gave a little nod of her head. "Let's begin now," I said firmly. "It does not make sense to wait until a house is available to begin the application process. We want to be prepared should a house become available." Our meeting came to an end as we exited Dan's office with a sheaf of papers in our hands.

That afternoon we embarked on the process of completing the complicated forms with their financial and personal questions. Indeed, it did take almost six months, but Dan nurtured us through the process. We filled out form after form, rewriting some answers when the forms were sent back to us with demands for further information. We made corrections, supplied financial data, copied tax information, added details for questions that needed clarification and generally complied with all the requirements of bureaucracy that needed to be observed. By the time the application for an FmHA loan was completed, we felt that the agency knew more about us than we did ourselves. The process had taken five months. Finally, the day of our interview arrived.

Our interviewer was a young man with a businesslike demeanor. But his bureaucratic position did not hinder him from being kind and supportive. "Welcome," he greeted us as we took our seats in his office. "I have all your paperwork before me. You did a good job of filling it out." It sounded to us as if he wanted us to qualify for the loan. We seemed to have passed the requirements demanded by our paperwork. Then came the question of our indebtedness. He asked, "Do you have any credit card debts?" As I replied, "No, we use our credit cards sparingly and pay our monthly bills promptly," Carolyn nodded her head in affirmation. Our interviewer looked down, consulting the papers before him on his desk. "I notice that you have a car," he said. "Do you owe anything on your automobile?" Carolyn and I answered together, "No." I added, "We have paid for our car already." He lifted his head and looked at us in surprise. "This is quite unusual. Do you have any debts?" I answered, "We cannot afford to have any debts. We don't owe anything except our monthly rent and the utility bills." "And," Carolyn added, "we owe our tithe to the Lord each week. But we pay that off monthly." He looked astounded and exclaimed, "That is remarkable! I don't believe that I have ever interviewed anyone who was debt free."

With that he proclaimed us qualified and instructed us to begin our house search from among the qualified FmHA houses that were currently available, warning us that such houses were in great demand and were snatched up very quickly by qualified families.

In the days following the interview, we learned of houses available in other parts of the county, but none near enough to Cottage Grove to make it a possibility. Hope alternated with disappointment. Even though they were not near us, the houses were being claimed almost immediately after they appeared on the market. Weeks went by.

Then, late on an August weekend, we received an excited phone call. It was Friday afternoon, and the caller was Dan Seleshanko. He had learned of a house that came on the market just that afternoon...and it was in Cottage Grove! Excitedly he said, "The people who were in line to buy the house have just received a raise in salary and are no longer qualified for an FmHA loan! This is a newly constructed house on a large lot. It is going to be listed tomorrow and will surely be taken in the first few minutes. Pick up your wife and meet me as quick as you can." Dan did not need to urge us to drop everything and meet him on the west side of town. As we drove to the destination at 265 South "R" Street, we discovered that the house was part of a newly developing neighborhood. In fact, the house was just in the process of completion.

Located on a large, deep lot that still needed landscaping, the house was in its final stages of completion. Dan awaited us with the front door key in his hand. As we made our tour of the interior, Dan explained that we could choose the color of the carpet and the color of the counter tops in the kitchen. The house was only one thousand eight square feet, with three small bedrooms and a single bath. The main room was barely large enough to accommodate a dining room table and living room furniture. The single car garage was as small as it could possibly be. But it had all the appearances of an elegant mansion to us. The undeveloped plot of ground upon which the house was built was fifty feet wide by 166 feet deep. Unfenced, the view extended all the way to the hills that rose a mile away.

As we stood on the street corner where we had parked our cars, Dan asked, "Well, what did you think of the house?" Carolyn was enthusiastic. "It is a lovely house. Even though it is a bit small, I can see our family living here." However, in my cautious timidity, I was hesitant to commit to the huge obligation of purchasing a house. "Let me think it over for a day or two. Home ownership is a big responsibility." Dan shook his head, "You don't have even one day. Tomorrow, this house will appear on the Multiple Listing Service, and I can guarantee you that when the real estate office opens, this house will be gone in the first few minutes. You have to make up your mind now." Carolyn agreed with him that such a nice house would vanish as soon as other realtors realized that it was available. "Percy, we prayed for a house to be available in our area, and this is it. Remember, it is the Lord who gave you the conviction last New Year's Day. And it is obviously the Lord who has brought Dan into our lives. And it certainly was the Lord who has seen us through application process. And this is a house that we can afford." Gesturing toward a new elementary school half a block away, she added, "It is only a mile and a half from the church and one block from the new elementary school that our children will now attend. They could walk to school!" I was convinced!

Dan took over. He encouraged us to write a check as earnest money to him right then and there. He explained his urgency, "As soon as I have your earnest money, I will drive directly to my office and post your earnest money against the multiple listing, and that will secure our priority in line for the new house. So I need a down payment now as earnest money to clinch the sale. Can you write me a check here and now? One hundred or two hundred dollars would be adequate."

I turned to Carolyn, who carried our check book in her purse. "Do we have two hundred dollars?" Carolyn, who paid our bills from our checking account, shook her head. "We don't have any money for a downpayment. I paid our bills, and we have virtually nothing left in our account." Dan asked, "Do you have any cash on you?" Carolyn had some loose change in her purse. I had a few bills in my wallet. Together, we managed to produce twenty-five dollars. As soon as we combined our money, Dan said, "I'll take it," reaching for our cash as if it were a million dollars. It never occurred to me then that the price of the earnest money was the same amount we had received as our first paycheck from the church. We prayed together on the street corner, thanking the Lord, and went our separate ways.

The following Monday we received a phone call from our realtor. Dan exclaimed, "The house is yours! But when the other realtors discovered that you reserved that house with only twenty-five dollars as earnest money, they went ballistic! They could have earned a good commission from the sale of that house. But now it is irretrievably yours." He did not mention that he forewent any commission himself to secure the house for us, a considerable sacrifice on his part. He chuckled, "Anyway, we used the money to get a credit check on you both, which you passed. So, for virtually nothing down, the Lord provided you a new house. Congratulations!"

We lived in that house for seven years until we moved to our next church in Oregon City. When the Farmer's Home Administration bought the house back from us, we realized a profit of several thousand dollars, enough to place a downpayment on another house in our new location. We also had enough money to add an extra bedroom and bath to our new home to accommodate our family.

Prior to our retirement from the active ministry, twenty-two years later, the mortgage on our house in Oregon City was paid in full. We finally had our own home, which was clearly the fulfillment of God's promise to meet all our needs. His ways are truly beyond our imagination!

21

Tiny Agents from God
August 1978

Money was tight in those early days of ministry in Cottage Grove. My gracious wife and I were deeply involved in the ministry of our small, struggling congregation. Our salary was still minimal, the economy poor, and frugality an ever-present necessity. While we were committed to tithing our meager income and also supporting missionary friends as our personal family missionaries, there seemed to be little money left for other things. So we were perplexed as to how we could participate in our church's Summer Camp Fund, a ministry to the children of our church whose parents could not afford to send them to summer camp. We did not have the money to donate. What little money remained in our check account would barely pay for the utility bills, which were due that week.

Wishing to donate to the camp fund which would help those children otherwise unable to attend summer camp, Carolyn and I had pledged ten dollars some weeks before, not knowing where the money would come from. Now it was the Sunday of collection. The ten dollars was due at the morning worship service. The thought nagged at the edges of my consciousness that we were unable to do our part in this worthy project while expecting others to do theirs. Carolyn and I determined to make up our part in some future week as a designated gift in the offering should we be unable to make our contribution on the official day of the camp offering.

As we were dressing for church, I happened to glance out the living room window, which afforded a panoramic view of the backyard. It was a pleasant view. Roses bloomed against the house just underneath the large picture window. A deep green lawn spread 30 feet out toward another flower bed, parallel with the back of the house and just below a modest open-rail fence. Beyond the small rail fence was the undeveloped section of our yard, stretching another 80 feet to the six-foot high cedar fence separating our property from the open area that stretched a mile to the base of the hills to the west. In that undeveloped area within our fence stood the children's swing set, complete with swings, slide and glider.

Ordinarily, it was a beautiful and peaceful scene. A leafy tree laden with large juicy red plums grew at one side of the yard, a discreet distance from the door of the equipment shed. Two new cedar fences reached down each side of the property from the house to the back propertyline. Thick white cotton-ball clouds dotted the powder blue sky. It was a perfect Sunday…except that we did not have the money to pay our pledge as we had promised.

However, something was out of balance. While I wear glasses and my vision is limited when it comes to focusing on items in the distance, I was positive that there was an indistinct, formless black shape hanging from the children's playground equipment. Calling to my wife, I asked, "Carolyn, what is that black blob hanging from the V-shaped legs of the swing set?" As she gazed out the window, I directed her attention. Pointing with my index finger, I commented, "It's over there on the right side. I don't recall seeing it yesterday. I can't quite make it out. Can you?" Carolyn squinted her eyes as if to focus more definitely. "I can't quite make it out," she repeated slowly, concentrating on the mysterious object. "We are almost late for church. Perhaps there is enough time for you to step out to investigate. Advancing into the backyard in my Sunday garb, I moved cautiously toward the swing set. A steady hum emanating from the moving black and yellow mass grew louder as I approached. Bees! It was a swarm of honey bees, looking for a new place to build their hive. Unaware at the time that swarming bees are not usually aggressive, I retreated rapidly to the safety of the house. In the living room, I announced my find to the family. Carolyn emphatically declared, "We have to deal with this situation now. I do not want bees in the same yard as our children when we return from church." I agreed. We were leaving for church in 15 minutes and had to deal with the situation before we exited the house. With three small children, we did not want to risk having bees and children in the same yard.

Frantically, we sought for a solution, all the time conscious of the pulsating black blob on our children's swing set. The phone book offered no solutions. Alerting 911 was not an option since this situation did not constitute an emergency. Almost by accident, we discovered our solution in the local newspaper, which was lying face down on the sofa, where it had been carelessly tossed. On the back page, in the classified ads, was an ad that held our solution. "Bees Wanted," the ad read in large black letters. In smaller print we read, "Will come and take your bees, $10 per hive. Please call…" A local phone number concluded the ad. A quick phone call settled the details. The beekeeper would come within an hour to secure the bees and would leave the money for us. Our three small children heard my closing comment, "Thank you for coming on such short notice. Will you please leave the ten dollars in an envelope and place it under the welcome mat at the front door? We will pick it up after church. Thank you very much. We appreciate your willingness to come on such short notice. Goodbye."

Borrowing ten dollars from our food budget to contribute to the summer camp fund, we confidently drove to church. At the proper time in our worship service, our contribution joined that of many other members of the church. At the end of the service, the chairman of the deacon board stood to announce that the Summer Camp Fund totaled enough to send all the children to camp, who had qualified by completing the list of memory verses from the Bible. It was a joyous occasion.

Following the service, Carolyn and I returned to our home with our children. As the car came to a halt in the driveway, our children opened the car doors and tumbled out. Running to the front door, they lifted the edge of the welcome mat to find an unmarked envelope hidden there. "It's here! It's here!" They jumped with excitement. Taking the envelope from our eldest daughter, I opened it to find inside a short note which read, "Thank you." Enclosed was a crisp ten-dollar bill. "The bees are gone," I announced a few moments later as we all stood at the picture window, looking out on our back yard. Then, because it was a teachable moment for our children, Carolyn added, "God knew that we needed ten dollars for the camp fund and so He sent those bees to our yard this very day. He didn't send too much or too little."

Indeed, it was unmistakably the provision of the Lord. Those tiny agents from God had provided the means for our contribution to the children's summer camp fund. We began to realize that the Lord delights in providing for our needs in incredibly creative ways.

The words of William Cowper's popular hymn are as true today as when he wrote them in 1774. "Deep in unfathomable mines of never failing skill He treasures up His bright designs and works His sov'reign will."

22

VIP Treatment
July 1980

Frugality can exact an invisible cost. Without being noticed, frugality can impart a mindset of poverty to those who practice it. The constant repetition of such statements as "We can't afford it," "It costs too much," or "It is beyond our means" can come to mean "We are undeserving of anything nice, for poverty is our lot in life." Keeping the economic rubber band stretched constantly can also subtly wear down the self-image of the one for whom economic prudence is a vital necessity. Quite unnoticed, this process of constant economic vigilance can become destructive to a healthy self-image. However, such destructiveness is not intended or ordained by the Lord. For need and want are really opportunities for an individual to trust the Lord for His provision, an opportunity for the one in need to look to the One who promises to meet our "needs" (necessities), not our "greeds" (selfish desires). And God's provision is abundant and generous, as illustrated by an episode we experienced at a national Conservative Baptist Annual Meeting in Anaheim, California.

"But we have a reservation!" We were standing in line at the five-star Anaheim Hilton Hotel and Convention Center. We had saved all year long in hopes of attending the Conservative Baptist National Meetings held in Anaheim that year. The hotel had extended a generously-reduced rate to the conference guests to entice business during the tourist off-season.

My wife, Carolyn, and I had made it a project of trust for the Lord to provide for our finances. Although our small church had placed a designated amount for pastoral conferences in its yearly budget, the amount was not adequate to cover expenses for pastor and wife. Carolyn and I were required to augment the registration fees, travel expenses and food costs from our own meager salary if we desired to attend the expensive meetings together. Even so, we felt that our attendance at the national meetings was part of our obligation as Conservative Baptists both to our CBA national fellowship and our local church. At the various conferences around the country, we attended workshops and plenary sessions geared to inspire and to motivate. We also enjoyed the fellowship of colleagues whom we saw only once a year. It was a spiritually refreshing time which we felt we needed to charge our spiritual batteries. So, it was that we had determined to make the financial sacrifice necessary to attend the meetings in Anaheim that year.

When we arrived at the huge 18-story hotel, we found the lobby crowded not only with conference guests but with tourists visiting various attractions in Southern California, the main attraction being Disneyland, a short distance to the north.

Winding our way through the large but crowded lobby, we joined one of the lines at the reservation desk. All the lines seemed to move slowly as Carolyn and I began to suspect that the hotel was faced with overcrowding. At the main desk we gave our names, stating that we were attendees at the Conservative Baptist Annual Meetings. "I am sorry, folks," the hotel receptionist replied. "We simply have no more rooms available. We are all filled up."

"But we have confirmed reservations for two, I objected. "Here are the papers that you mailed to us in confirmation a month ago." As we produced the file, his expression changed.

"Oh! I am sorry," he exclaimed as he reviewed the pages of our reservation confirmation form. "We will try to work something out. Either we will find lodging for you here, or we will locate accommodations for you at a nearby hotel. Would you mind waiting for a half hour while we try to work this out?" "Not at all," I replied as courteously as I could, hiding my growing frustration and anxiety. I thought to myself, *"We have waited in a long line, produced confirmed reservations, and still are not able to get a room? How much more frustrating can it get?"* As we made our way from the reception desk, we noticed others like us in the crowded lobby. Obviously, they were also waiting for a room assignment. It was easy to spot them among the crush of people the ones with worried expressions of their faces.

Waiting in the huge lobby of the hotel while people swirled around us in the frenzy of getting their room assignments and struggling with their luggage, we heard snippets of various conversations. One couple came away from the desk with huge smiles on their faces. "Oh, our room assignment is on the 8th floor. We ought to have a great view of Disneyland." Another man returned from the registration desk to his wife, who was guarding their luggage. "Honey, I just saw our room, and it is elegant!" Happily, they made their way toward the elevators. It was hard not to envy them.

As the minutes dragged by, we heard others with more alarming comments. "It's incredible! They ran out of rooms! With our kids, we are being assigned to the hotel down the street." From another couple, "We had to settle for a room with double beds. They had nothing left." With each negative comment, we felt that our chances of remaining in this elegant hotel were diminishing. We felt sure that we would have to settle for a disagreeable alternative some distance away, creating the additional inconvenience of having to make a stressful commute each morning through congested Southern California traffic. As the half hour of waiting expired, we approached the desk with a vague sense of trepidation.

The desk clerk shook his head sadly and said, "We are sorry for the mix up. You did have a confirmed reservation." Then he smiled and added, "The Tower has a few free rooms on the VIP floor. We could put you both in a room there. You would simply have to use the tower elevator that goes to the upper floors." Handing us the electronic keys to our room, he smiled again and added, "We are sorry for the inconvenience. We hope that you will enjoy your new accommodations. If you have any complaints, please speak to the concierge in the lounge on the 18th floor. And please use the special Tower elevator. It is the only one that will take you to the top floor of our hotel."

Considerably heartened, we dragged our luggage to the tower elevator and punched the button labeled "18." It was the topmost button. Swiftly we were borne upward, and in a few seconds the doors slid open to an astonishing sight.

Across the hall from the elevator was a very wide entrance into a large, elegantly-decorated lounge room with floor-to-ceiling windows that looked north to Disneyland and to the distant Sierra Madre mountain range beyond. A very large table was laden with artistically prepared appetizers, tasty light snacks, various assortments of candies, and both soft and hard drinks. It was the VIP Lounge reserved for Very Important People, the guests of the 18th floor. Just inside the doorway sat the concierge at a small but ornately-carved desk. He smiled warmly at us and asked for our room number. Upon receiving it, he directed us down the hall to our room and assured us of his availability for any needs we might discover.

The room was one of the nicest hotel rooms that we had experienced up to that time. Two king-sized beds occupied less than half the space in the room. A desk with a comfortable straight chair invited us to do whatever clerical work we might have. A plush lounge chair faced the large screen TV. There was also a round breakfast table with two expensively upholstered chairs. A generous chest of drawers with a huge mirror completed the bedroom ensemble. The bathroom facilities were first-rate, appearing to have been newly remodeled.

The beds were turned down on each side, ready for occupancy. On the counterpane were two chocolates wrapped in gold foil. Opening the large closet door, we found two new, white terrycloth robes. The spacious closet accommodated all our clothes as well as our luggage.

The view of the city was stunning from our elevation. In the distance the crystal-clear Sierra Madre mountain range presented a gray-green background to the spacious view of Anaheim and Garden Grove. It was obvious to us that this room with its grand view was far more expensive than our reservations merited. After settling in with our belongings, we returned to the VIP lounge. There we encountered a number of our colleagues, who had also been displaced due to the overwhelming crush of guests and had been reassigned to the VIP floor in the hotel tower.

We noticed that they carried small plastic plates with a variety of tasty foods prepared by the hotel chef especially for the guests in the VIP lounge. I reached for a plate when Carolyn asked, "Are we supposed to be here in the VIP lounge, helping ourselves to the goodies obviously prepared for hotel VIP's?" Assuming the air of a wealthy patron, I replied, "Of course! We are housed on this floor, and this room is for the residents of this floor." Carolyn responded, "But we did not pay for that fancy of a room, and this floor is for very important persons. We are not really supposed to be here."

Summoning my theology, I asked my puzzled wife, "Are you saved?" Startled by the question, she said, "Yes, of course!"

I countered, "Do you deserve heaven?" Carolyn, ever the conservative with a biblical understanding of the Gospel, did not hesitate to answer. "No, but Jesus died for me, so I will be with Him in Heaven."

"Exactly," I concluded. "We don't deserve to be on this floor either, but the hotel made it possible for us to be housed here with all the rights and privileges of those who are staying in the Tower. We have been granted the privileges of being VIP's during our days here. Let's enjoy it and make the most of the privilege."

Our stay at the Anaheim Hilton was both comfortable and enjoyable. We did not have to pay for any food that week because the VIP lounge offered a variety of free foods fit for the morning, midday and evening meals. The magnificent views from large windows were spellbinding, and the hotel service was geared to our every comfort.

We decided that this was a clear lesson concerning God's grace. We may not have deserved such high-class treatment, but someone had made it possible for us to enjoy the pleasures of the top floor. So also with our eternal destiny; while we do not deserve heaven, our Lord Jesus Christ paid the price with His own blood so that we (by faith in Him) could enjoy the everlasting joys of eternity's "Top Floor."

23

"Nothing Religious!"
August 1980

"We have a difficult situation here and need your help." Doug Lund, the director at the only funeral home in our town of Cottage Grove, was on the other end of the phone line. An easy and relaxed friendship had sprung up between us after I had conducted three funerals in the first three weeks after my arrival as a new pastor in town. Now he felt free to ask me to preside at funerals that had difficult circumstances surrounding them. Several other ministers in town simply did not conduct funerals to his satisfaction. Further shrinking the pastoral pool were those who, because of denominational restrictions, could not conduct funerals outside of their parishes. However, I saw those difficult funerals as opportunities to administer the grace of God to hurting people and more significantly as opportunities to preach the saving message of the Lord Jesus. Apparently my approach met with Doug Lund's approval, for, he called me whenever there were funerals that demanded special skill. I suspected even then that Doug understood that I needed whatever "extra" revenue could be earned by taking on wider responsibilities. Indeed, the exposure that I had to various segments of the non-religious community gave me a unique opportunity to share the Gospel with those who might not have heard it.

Doug filled me in on the situation. "A middle-aged woman died of asphyxiation in her automobile. She apparently committed suicide." He went on to fill in the details. "The police have pieced together a probable story from the details offered by the husband. The husband and wife had gone out on the town. They had been drinking rather heavily and got into a nasty argument as they drove home. After driving the car into the garage, he angrily left her to get out of the car by herself. Entering the house alone, he wearily lay down on a sofa and almost immediately dropped off into a drunken sleep. Apparently, his wife, possibly thinking that she would command his attention with some dramatic act, started the engine of the automobile after finding a piece of garden hose, which she fastened from her window to the exhaust pipe, and sat back in the car with the windows closed as much as possible, considering that the hose was pinched between the window and the window frame. Since he was asleep inside the house, he never returned to investigate her absence, and she died in what might have been a tragic drunken bid for sympathy. He made it clear when we were making the arrangements that he and his wife were not church-going people. And he was emphatic that he was not interested in a religious funeral. Still, would you be willing to take on this situation?" Doug Lund paused, awaiting my answer.

As a pastor in the community, I felt an obligation never to turn down an opportunity to share the Gospel with others, so I accepted the difficult assignment. After the funeral director made a phone call to the newly bereaved man, I called upon him in his home.

When the door opened, I greeted a large man, casually but expensively attired, who invited me into his home. He was neither cordial nor unfriendly. Rather he seemed cautious, not knowing what to expect from a minister. He offered me a seat opposite his recliner in a room that was tastefully decorated, unlike the humble furnishings of a working-class home. It was obvious that money was no stranger in this home. After a few sentences of small talk about the weather, geared to break the ice, he leaned forward toward me. Extending his hand and pointing to a large ring on his finger, he asked in a confidential tone, "Are you a brother?" Not knowing what he meant, I peered at the design of the ring and suddenly realized that it was a Mason's ring. "I am a 32nd degree

Mason," he continued rather proudly. Repeating himself, he asked again, "Are you a brother?" I shook my head and smiled. "No, I'm not," I replied. Immediately, it seemed that an invisible wall arose between us.

"Look," he began, "Let me make it clear; I don't want anything religious!" As he spoke, he kept his grief well controlled. Adamantly he emphasized, "My wife and I are not church-goers. So keep religion out of it."

I countered, "But death is a reality beyond our control. And the Bible has a great deal to say about life and death. Don't you want me to speak the truth?" He shook his head in disagreement. After letting him know that I was a minister of the Gospel and that my funeral services were necessarily "religious," I arose and walked to the door. With my hand on the knob, I turned and said very kindly, "Perhaps I am not the person you want. I will be glad to consult with the funeral director and have him recommend someone else better suited for your purposes. I want you to be satisfied with the person who conducts something as important to you as this."

As I turned the knob and opened the door, he said, "No, no, wait a minute. You seem to be an honest man. You are the one I want."

Still, throughout our subsequent contacts prior to the funeral service, he remained aloof. It was as if he was disassociating himself from the planning of the service. When I asked about details of his wife's life, he simply directed me to the brief obituary printed in the local paper two days after her death. It presented a difficulty that complicated funeral preparations. I could never simply read an impersonal funeral service as a formality, for I truly desired to minister comfort to bereaved families. One of the basic purposes in my funeral services was to handle the life details of the deceased with gentleness and dignity. This required that I interview members of the family to familiarize myself with their lost loved one. But in this case, it was nearly impossible since the widower was the only person who could supply me with those personal details, and he was removed from the process by his own choice. I found myself praying and pondering how to present the Gospel in the funeral service in such a clear and palatable way as to insure effective communication without alienating the grieving man. But the way seemed to escape me.

One evening, just a day before the scheduled funeral, I called on the man once again. As I rang his doorbell, the noise of a party greeted me. Essentially, a "wake" was taking place. When he answered the chiming of the doorbell with a drink in his hand, he curtly dismissed me, saying, "See my sons in the back bedroom. I don't have time to see you now." Slightly put off by his abrupt manner, I edged my way through a crowd of people, drinks in hand, who seemed to be friends and relatives of the recently widowed man. I walked down a short hallway and turned into a bedroom, discovering three young men in their 20's standing with their young wives, apparently escaping the raucous revelry in the other room. After introducing myself, I asked if there was anything that they wanted me to include in the funeral ceremony.

One of the sons said, "Our mother taught us a verse of the Bible. Perhaps you could use it. But I can't remember what it was." Another son added, "Is there a book of 'John' in the Bible? I think that it was a verse from that book." I asked eagerly, "Was it John 3:16? 'For God so loved the world that he gave his only begotten Son, that whosoever believeth in him should not perish, but have everlasting life.'" "No." They all shook their heads at that unfamiliar verse. The third son remembered, "I think that it started 'Ye must...'" and then faltered into silence. I asked, "Was it John 3:3, 'Ye must be born again'?" "Yes!" they all chorused in remembrance. "That's it! Will you use that verse in your service?" Inwardly rejoicing, I assured them, "Of course!"

At the funeral service the next day, following a scripture reading, a prayer for comfort in the face of death, and words of encouragement to the family, I presented the Gospel on the basis of John 3:3, beginning, "The family has asked me to share with you a verse that they had learned from their mother, and I am always glad to do what the family asks.

140

It is in answer to the question, 'How do we prepare for the moment of death?'" The following moments contained a clear presentation of the imperative of being born again spiritually by accepting the Lord Jesus by faith. I gave my personal testimony and a discreet invitation to join me in a quiet prayer of acceptance of Christ. Following the service, the husband of the deceased roughly grasped my hand and said with some emotion, "Good service! Thanks." The sons and their wives were equally appreciative.

On my way home, I remembered Proverbs 3:5-6 which commands us, "Trust in the LORD with all thine heart; and lean not unto thine own understanding. In all thy ways acknowledge Him, and He shall direct thy paths."

God had clearly provided a way for the Gospel to be preached in answer to my prayer!

24

The Bar Crowd
August 1980

They stood in the "parlor" of the funeral home, perhaps 18 of them -- unpretentious, dressed in casual clothes, their lined faces testifying to a hard life lived on the fringes of society. They were not the typically well-dressed group of people that usually attended funerals in that town. In this case, their friend had just passed away suddenly while at the bar, and now the group from a local tavern had come to remember him and to deal with his rather unexpected demise.

Doug Lund, the funeral director, had called me earlier in the week, asking if I would be willing to conduct a funeral for an alcoholic who died, penniless, of a heart attack and of cirrhosis of the liver. He explained that the subject of the funeral was one of those "forgotten people," the kind that isn't noticed by passersby on the street. He was a long time "regular" at a local tavern and over the years had made friends of a small group of people who were also patrons of that establishment. With no wife or children, he had no other known relatives with whom he was still in contact. In fact, none of the friends from the tavern knew of the existence of any extended family. They had taken a modest collection to help defray the costs of his burial. Doug Lund made it clear to me over the phone that I would not be receiving any remuneration for my services. In fact, he, himself, was offering his services free of charge. The collection would barely cover the costs of a cemetery plot.

Beside our professional connection, Doug and I had developed a personal friendship. He and his staff seemed to approve of my approach to conducting funeral services. While I did not compromise the presentation of the Gospel at funerals or at memorial services, neither did I force "religion" upon the grieving mourners. It was my conviction that a funeral service was an opportunity to lovingly minister the grace and comfort of God to people who were shocked and traumatized in the face of death, a force not under human control, and obviously much stronger than the mortal grip on life. So I made every effort to handle the memory of the life just ended with sympathy and dignity, to focus upon the lasting values espoused by the deceased which were left as a legacy to those who remained behind.

My presentation of the Gospel at the end of the service was in the form of a personal testimony rather than a forceful preaching message with a confrontational public invitation. It was low-key, designed to allow grieving people the freedom to consider the claims of Christ in the privacy of their own hearts.

This funeral service presented some difficulties for me. While it was my usual practice to interview the remaining family members prior to the actual service to learn about the life and interests of the deceased and to collect information about birth, marriage, children, employment, and the significant experiences of life, in this case there was nothing to learn. His friends at the bar knew nothing about him except that he lived alone and was dependent upon the largess of society. He received welfare from the state but managed to drink away a good portion of that income. What they knew of him was clouded through the haze of his alcoholic fog.

Armed with a rather standard funeral ceremony taken from one of my funeral manuals and adapted for the occasion, I arrived the morning of the scheduled funeral to find the funeral director in a state of uncertainty and anxiety. Doug greeted me, "I think we have a problem. My associate just notified me that the friends of the deceased have just arrived, but they refuse to enter the large room set aside for services." "Why? What's the problem?" "I don't know," Doug replied. "But they seem to be uneasy. I think that this is an unfamiliar place for most of them. Probably most of them have not been closely associated with death." We were interrupted by Doug's associate, who had just returned from the "parlor," where the group had gathered. It was a large area between the outer door of the establishment and the main room, where services were conducted. Dotted with lamp tables, overstuffed chairs and comfortable sofas, the décor succeeded in conveying an atmosphere of casual comfort. However, it was not designed to conduct formal funeral or memorial services. "They are not moving into the main room. I think that the presence of the casket in the main room is intimidating them. What are we going to do?" He shrugged in resignation. "I don't know what more we can do." Doug Lund, a compassionate and experienced funeral director, turned to me and said, "Let's see if you can encourage them to move into the main room. Can you motivate them to move?" I asked, "Can you change the arrangement of the main room? Perhaps the casket and flowers are overwhelming to them." The associate protested, "We can't move the casket now. The room is already set up with the casket, flowers, seating, and lectern. If they won't move there, where will we conduct the service?" "Let me try," I said, walking out of the office into the hallway leading to parlor.

As I came upon the group, I notice their unease. Mainly men, there were a few women in the group. None were in their youth. But drink had taken its toll on most of them. The women showed facial wrinkles that should have been associated with those much older than they. Large red veins in the faces of some of the men testified to their long acquaintance with alcohol. It was immediately obvious to me that they did not know what to expect and were quite wary. It was equally obvious that they would not be persuaded to move into a room with a casket containing a dead body.

Originally not knowing what kind of group I would be serving, I had dressed in a suit and tie earlier that morning, standard dress for a minister conducting a funeral. Aware now, that my very clothes separated me from these who were gathered in memory of their friend, I took off my coat and removed my tie, placing them on the back of a padded chair nearby. Unbuttoning the top button of my white shirt, I rolled back the cuffs of my sleeves. They watched in silence. Further taking in the situation, I quickly realized that reading a traditional funeral service would not do. Even my Bible and notebook seemed to intimidate them. The black Bible and leather-covered notebook, which contained my funeral service notes, I casually laid on a lamp table while introducing myself to them.

Realizing that these people were "out of their element," I invited the ladies to sit in the comfortable upholstered chairs and padded sofas scattered in the parlor setting of the funeral home. Some of the men leaned against the wall, while others settled down in the folding chairs that the funeral director and his associate hastily brought into the area.

I began in a casual manner. "Let's lay aside the formal stuff and spend a few moments just talking to each other. Your friend (I mentioned the deceased by name) must have been a pretty good man for all of you to come out to honor him at his funeral." Some of the ladies wiped away tears. Some of the men nodded their heads in agreement with my assessment. "So, since I didn't know him, why don't you tell me what he was like?" There followed some moments of silence. Then one man cleared his throat and began, "I'm the bartender, and I knew him for several years." He went on to describe the generous nature of the deceased. Others began to speak. One by one they shared anecdotes of their friend. At times we all laughed. At other times the women wept while some of the men brought out handkerchiefs or tissues with which to wipe their eyes.

When it seemed that the sharing time was over, I said, "Look, I know that none of us want to be here. This is not as pleasant as the fellowship around a few drinks. But I do want to share something pretty important with you." And I began to explain the Gospel in as plain a language as

I could, quoting pertinent verses from Scripture that I had memorized long ago. I gave my personal testimony of accepting Jesus into my heart at the age of eight and what it meant to be forgiven. I concluded by saying, "I'm going to pray the prayer that I had prayed when I was eight years old, accepting Jesus into my heart. If you want to pray it quietly in your own heart, I'll go slowly so you can repeat my words. Do so only if you are sincere." Then I prayed the simple prayer that I had prayed as a child. "Dear Lord Jesus, I know that I am a sinner. I am sorry for my sin. Please forgive me. Come into my heart and take control of my life. Thank you for saving me. Amen." It was not a sophisticated prayer but a sincere, heartfelt sentiment.

When my prayer ended, I concluded with a statement to the group, "You don't have to be religious. But you do have to let the Lord Jesus have control of your life if you wish to live beyond physical death. If you do surrender your life to the Lord Jesus, you'll never regret it." It was not a high-powered invitation, but it was an opportunity for some in that group to accept the Lord. I then closed in prayer, thanking the Lord for faithful friends like those who came to honor the life of their friend. Inwardly, I hoped that someone had accepted the Lord.

Following the service, a lady with the marks of a hard-lived life came up to me and declared with tears of gratitude, "Thank you for your words. When I die, I hope you will have my funeral." Her sincerity moved me. However, it did not happen. I left the community shortly after that, responding to the call of another church.

But God had fully provided for my need in conducting a funeral for a man I did not know and about whom I knew nothing, and the opportunity to present the Gospel to a most unlikely group was a great privilege. And God had planned a quick adjustment for me to meaningfully communicate with them. Only God knows of the hearts that were changed at that informal service. Perhaps after my death I may meet someone in eternity who accepted Christ Jesus that day.

25

After Many Days
December 1980

It is simply known as "Keil and Delitsch," a set of critical commentaries (dealing with the Hebrew Old Testament). Critical commentaries as opposed to devotional commentaries, tend to be quite expensive. The 25-volume set (now no longer available in that edition) cost more than three times the $100 I had already saved. My wife and I were ministering in a small church in an isolated logging community on the Interstate 5 corridor which ran north and south through the western side of the state of Oregon. It should not have surprised us (as it did) that the church was unable to support a pastor financially. They had represented themselves as being self- supporting when, in fact, they were deeply indebted and very close to folding financially. With the priorities of food and lodging, utilities and health care, it was virtually impossible for me to save money to augment my small reference library. However, I strongly felt that it was essential to build a reference library since there was no theological library within eighty miles of our town. I carefully saved small bits of change whenever I could, hoping that within a year or two I could afford to order that set of books. As I pored over various catalogs and book advertisements, I planned my next purchase, "The Ante-Nicene Fathers," which presented all the writings of the early church fathers before the Council of Nicaea (325 A.D.). Far from any theological library, it was vital to have at hand the tools for deeper Bible study and sermon preparation.

However, the Lord had other plans.

Why the honor was bestowed upon me to be asked to join the Board of Trustees of the financially needy Judson Baptist College I do not know. However, I responded to the invitation positively, unsure of my qualifications to be part of a group of successful and influential businessmen. Apparently, I was to be the token clergyman on the board as required by school policy. The college's financial crisis was not an unfamiliar experience for me, for I was facing economic pressures at home as well as financial issues at the church.

Not long after joining the board of the college, I was asked to give as sacrificially as I could from my personal finances to help the school survive its monetary crisis. My wife and I did not have anything to give from our household budget -- nothing, that is, except my laboriously accumulated library fund. It had taken me over a year to accumulate the $100 designated as my "library fund." To give that away to the college would erase the anticipation of ever being able to add to my small (and, I felt, inadequate) library. It was a fierce inner struggle. I had worked diligently to save that money. My goal was still beyond the horizon, for it would take me years to purchase books that I needed if I was to continue to minister in remote locations away from adequate biblical resources. Yet, as I wrestled with my conscience, the Lord spoke to me with an inner prompting. The voice inside of me seemed to be saying, "Give it all to Me." Finally, I surrendered. After consulting with my gracious and very supportive wife, I contributed all my book money in a single gift to the college. My dreams for an adequate pastor's library vanished in one single gesture as I laid an envelope on the table at the next board meeting. Strangely, as my library dreams vanished, I did not feel depressed. Rather, a firm conviction pervaded my soul that I had done the right thing.

In the ensuing months, I laid aside the aims for expanding my small library and plunged into the ministry of our small church without any regrets, using whatever references I had for Bible study. Since computers were still too expensive for my personal consideration, online sermon study resources were not available to me. Further, I was totally computer illiterate.

But the Lord had not forgotten.

Two years later, as Carolyn and I opened a Christmas card from a former high school student to whom we had ministered in a former church almost ten years before, a surprise awaited us. Now a successful medical doctor, our former Sunday school student wrote a note of appreciation about our ministry to him so many years ago and included a check for $3,000 to be used in the ministry of the church. It was with joy that I shared the news with our church board and presented them with the check.

One board member said suddenly, "I move that we give $1,000 to Pastor Kooshian for his library. He has not been able to buy books for all the time he has been here. And if it were not for his ministry to this doctor, we would not be receiving this check at all." The board heartily agreed and approved the motion. As the deacon board deliberations were made public to the church, the church body generously and enthusiastically approved the board's action. With the money, I was able not only to buy the original "Keil and Delitsch" set of volumes, but the "Ante-Nicene Fathers" set (and several other single reference volumes) as well.

Investing in the Lord is never a bad decision. We cannot outgive God, Who honors acts of generosity and sacrifice. The proverb of Solomon, the ancient king of Israel (and the wisest man who ever lived) is still true. "Cast thy bread upon the waters: for thou shalt find it after many days." (Ecclesiastes 11:1)

26

A Comforting Arm
January 1990

By their very nature, times of crisis cannot only create great fear, but they can also serve as opportunities to grow in faith. That thought opens the Book of James in the New Testament.

One of my favorite paraphrases of Scripture is the J.B. Phillips "Letters to Young Churches" (1947 McMillen Brothers). The Book of James begins with the following passage:

"When all kinds of trials and temptations crowd into your lives my brothers, don't resent them as intruders, but welcome them as friends! Realize that they come to test your faith and to produce in you the quality of endurance. But let the process go on until that endurance is fully developed, and you will find you have become men of mature character with the right sort of independence." (James 1:2-4)

Without being conscious of it, I was under incredible stress. Carolyn and I had been called from our church in Cottage Grove to the Victory Baptist Church in Oregon City. This church was recovering from an acrimonious split that had occurred over a year before Carolyn and I arrived on the scene. The compassionate ministry of the interim pastor helped little. He was an excellent leader, but the wounds of the congregation ran deep and red. I soon found out that the church was like a battlefield where the smoke had not cleared and where the wounded were moaning and crying out for help. While these wounds were not apparent on the surface, it did not take much investigation to reveal the enormity of the hurt and dysfunction of the congregation.

The former pastor apparently was not skilled or educated enough to lead a congregation successfully. So when he publicly exposed an incestual relationship within the church at the close of a Mother's Day service, he immediately shocked the women of the church and created two factions within the congregation. One faction was outraged that such sin had occurred within the church and demanded swift discipline upon the victimizer. The victim was humiliated. The perpetrator went to jail.

The other faction was outraged that the revelation had occurred on Mother's Day. They were affronted at the handling of the whole affair, demanding the immediate resignation of the pastor. At a tumultuous meeting of the church the leadership resigned and left the church, forsaking a now leaderless congregation. One would have concluded wrongly that in a church split, the remaining people would be unified. Not so in this church. While many left the church and scattered to other nearby congregations, there remained people on both sides of the issue who had been damaged by the severity of the crime, the mishandling of the situation, and the betrayal of the leadership who had left the church.

Each faction fiercely opposed the other. The interim pastor barely held things together, as the two strong factions continued to battle each other for leadership. Although I had a superficial knowledge of the history of the church, I was unprepared to face the severity and deep-seated hostility of various members of the congregation. The wounds were so deep for some members that they sought professional counselling to cope with their inner damage.

In my candidate message to the church, I preached on forgiveness from II Corinthians 9:8. After reading the text, "And God is able to make all grace abound toward you; that ye, always having all sufficiency in all things, may abound to every good work," I stated my theme that believers have received such generous grace and forgiveness from God that they have plenty of forgiveness to share with others. Two families walked out of the room. The Deacon Board of the church confronted me after the service. Shocked, they informed me that my message had offended two families who were determined never to return. All I could say in my defense was that I was committed to preaching the Word of God. Despite the incident, the church voted overwhelmingly to call us as their pastoral family.

However, the war for power did not decrease. Those who could not heal from their wounds, and those who would not heal, preferred outrage rather than wholeness. They preferred the role of the offended. One faction approved of me as the only hope for the church. The other faction opposed me because they were losing power and influence within the church body. Business meetings became battlefields, so that the congregation inevitably began to lose members. As each member family left, the adult parents in the family made sure to inflict as much pain on the pastor and congregation as possible. As I tried to encourage and reason with those who strove to gain power, I was rejected by their resistance and hardness of heart.

One of the leaders of the dissident faction in the church was a very large man without an ounce of fat upon him. His incredibly fit physique bore silent witness that he was a sportsman. So it was no surprise when I learned that he had been a professional football player and was now coaching at a local high school as well as being involved in community sports. Unfortunately for me, he and his wife had made it publicly known that they opposed the pastor and sought for his resignation. Gently approaching them, I entreated, "Please don't be offended at my ministry. I am not your enemy. I really appreciate you and hope that we can work together for the good of the church and the glory of the Lord." When I sensed an unbending hostility, I asked, "Does it bother you when I speak openly with you?" With an unbending reserve, the wife replied, "It bothers me very much!"

Not long after, the leader of the dissident faction knocked on my office door. Immediately after my invitation to enter, I sensed that something was very wrong. Yet I smiled and greeted him, calling him by name. Silently, he entered and took his seat across the desk. Without a word, he opened the large Bible which he had been carrying. Without removing his gaze from me, he pulled a new pencil from his pocket. Staring into my eyes, he reversed the pencil in his hand and tapped the eraser on the pages of his open Bible. Narrowing his eyes, he finally spoke while still tapping on his Bible with the pencil eraser. "What I want to know…" He paused dramatically, his unblinking eyes fixed upon mine. The tapping of his pencil on the pages of his Bible was the only sound breaking the silence in the room. Finally he finished his sentence, "…is whether the decisions you are making for this church are really based on the Bible." He leaned forward, his somber expression, almost grim, remaining fixed upon his face.

Perhaps I should have been intimidated by such an aggressive encounter. Certainly, in my more youthful and inexperienced years, I might not have had the fortitude to withstand such a threatening confrontation. However, after years of exposure to the manipulative tactics of adult behavior, I had learned not to buckle under the intense pressure put upon me by those who supposed me to be weak and vulnerable. Instead, the prayer crossed my mind, *"Lord, do I have to put up with this kind of intimidation?"* From somewhere inside of me, came an answer.

My mouth tightened as I turned without a word to select the largest Bible I could find on the library shelf behind me. Turning back to the desk, I opened it, reached into the desk drawer and selected a new pencil. Now, fixing my eyes upon his, I began to tap on my Bible with the eraser end of the pencil. Silently I bored my gaze into his eyes for a few moments. Now the tapping sound in the office was from my pencil. Finally, I spoke. "Yes! Yes, I am," I answered. "Now…" I paused for a moment, then continued, "Which decision is it that you want to question?" I sat back and waited patiently for his reaction.

He looked startled. "Well, no, no." He shook his head quickly in a negative shiver. "There wasn't any particular decision that I was questioning," he added rather defensively. Hastily closing his Bible and gathering his pencil, he rose and moved toward the office door, items in hand. "I just wanted to know…" His voice trailed off as he went out the door. I was not elated but rather saddened by the episode.

Eventually my stress levels rose. Finally, I suffered a stress attack which took me to the emergency room of the local hospital.

Our family physician, a fine Christian man, examined me later at the clinic where we received our medical care. He diagnosed me with high blood sugar and an imbalance of rest and exercise. The official diagnosis was diabetes. Addressing my stress attack, he concluded, "Your stress is not necessarily a matter of ungodliness or lack of faith. It is of organic imbalance." Prescribing medication and a regimen of diet and exercise, he released me.

However, shortly after, I suffered a heart attack. The local hospital was ill-equipped to handle heart patients. However, on that evening, a very competent cardiologist who practiced in a neighboring town just happened to be in the hospital, visiting one of his patients. As he heard the emergency call, he hurried to the emergency room and took over my care. With a shot of Streptokinase, a wonder drug, all the blood clots in my heart dissolved within a matter of seconds. After an examination in his office some days later, he discovered the location of the original cardiac obstruction and scheduled me for an angioplasty. The procedure was a success, and I was soon actively engaged in the ministry again. But the stresses continued. The opposition remained relentless.

One late afternoon during my recovery, I stood in the center of our family room gazing at the beautiful sunset. Colorful hues of every shade painted the western sky. In spite of the beauty before my eyes, a profound sadness filled my heart. As I contemplated the hardness and rejection on the part of some of the congregation I could not see any way out. The ministry was far more difficult than I had ever imagined. Under these circumstances, I could not lead the church into spiritual health. And it was clearly taking a serious toll on my personal health. In the quietness of my heart, I cried out in despair, "Lord, they are killing me."

I did not anticipate what happened next. Perhaps I expected the Lord to chide me, telling me to buck up and take it like a man. Or perhaps the Lord would scold me for buckling under pressure. I recalled the admonition from Hebrews 12:3, "For consider Him that endured such contradiction of sinners against Himself, lest ye be wearied and faint in your minds." Feelings of failure washed over me.

Suddenly I sensed a presence beside me. It was as if some invisible being had placed his arm around my shoulders. As I wondered at this impression, into my mind entered the words, "I know how you feel, Percy. I suffered, too." I do not pretend to believe in special revelation other than the 66 books of the Bible. However, I do believe in Jesus Christ. I only know that at that moment, I became comforted and encouraged by those words.

From that point on, the tangle of hostile members of the church began to unravel. As resistant members left the church, other positive believers came to join the fellowship. Slowly, the church began to regain spiritual health.

There were no easy solutions. But with the influx of new members and a few new believers, God rescued our church from dissolving into hostility and animosity. The poison of disunity disappeared as members of the dissident faction left the church. I learned that not all defections from the church constituted a loss. As the church became united, its vision increased. Soon we were in a building project as we looked forward to church growth.

Even in adversity and health crises, I learned that in Jesus there is not only provision for the body but also solace and peace for the soul. "Thou wilt keep him in perfect peace, whose mind is stayed on thee: because he trusteth in thee" (Isaiah 26:3)

27

The Lord's Lathe
June 1997

"And this is the lathe." The teacher in our seventh-grade woodshop class was orienting his students on the first day of the semester to the various power tools arrayed in the work area of the large room. "You can turn all kinds of wood into round and tubular shapes. It is even possible to shape bowls out of decorative wood burls." Our introductory tour included drill presses, table saws, planers, jointers, and sanders. All the tools were fascinating, and I looked forward to using each of them. However, of all the tools, the wood-lathe fascinated me the most. It is a simple stationary power tool that allows a person to shape square blocks of wood into beautiful round turnings -- gavels, pens, bowls, candlesticks, rolling pins, bedposts, etc. I imagined myself turning intricate wood objects that would be the wonder of all who viewed them. Alas, it was not to be. The lathe was a tool for the more advanced wood class and I never advanced to that class. However, my imaginary romance with the wood lathe never left the recesses of my mind.

It was not until forty years later, in my first ministry as pastor, that I became engaged in the pleasures of wood working again. Tom Douglas, our deacon board chairman and woodshop teacher at the local high school, asked, "What do you do for recreation?" observing my stress in the ministry at the church. "You need a hobby, or you will break under the demands of our church. We aren't paying you a living wage. We've got some very difficult people here, and our church is deeply in debt. You need a relaxing hobby! Why don't you take an evening adult-education class in wood-working at the high school? It's fun, easy, and very inexpensive. And I teach it." It was an offer I could not resist. During my pleasant hours in the woodshop, I renewed my desire for a wood-lathe.

A few years later, God supplied an antique from a secondhand store at the Oregon coast. Carolyn and I were invited to spend two days visiting our colleagues, Dennis and Carole Stevenson in Coos Bay, Oregon. The first evening after dinner, Dennis suggested, "Why don't we go out on my boat into the bay tomorrow and look for clams?" Carolyn and I had never engaged in such an activity, even though we both loved clams. Dennis informed us that the Empire Clams (also known as "horse-neck" clams) were magnificent, and the experience of digging for them was exciting and enjoyable. Certainly, it was a new adventure for Carolyn and myself. "We've never done it before," I replied, "but we sure are willing to try." Carole chimed in, "It's fun. You will really enjoy it once you get used to harvesting them. We will provide the pails for carrying the clams. Since we don't have enough shovels, you can just use your hands to dig through the sand." The excitement of a new adventure kept me awake for a while that night before sleep overtook me.

Early the next morning, at low tide, we sailed out to the sand bars in the bay, muddy underwater sand dunes mixed with the detritus of the sea. Others had already arrived in a variety of boats to secure their quota of the giant clams.

Armed only with pails, we followed Carole's instructions. "When you see a hole the size of your forefinger, stick your finger in the hole. Nothing will bite or sting you. When you feel something pull away from you, you will know that it is the neck of the clam. Dig quickly about 8 to 12 inches down and you will find the clamshell." It proved to be an exciting experience for Carolyn and me. Soon we had quite a few clams in our pails. Unfortunately, the broken shells and the grit of the sand exacted their toll on our fingertips, for in the excitement of discovering the Empire Clams in the cold sand and water, we did not feel the scratches and abrasions accumulating on our fingers.

We were so engrossed in the excitement of our new adventure that we did not notice that our small boat had slipped its anchor and was drifting away into the deep water of the bay. With the possibility of being stranded on the sand with the rising tide, we were in a potentially dangerous situation. "Hey, Dennis," I frantically called out, "your boat is drifting out into the bay!" Others on the sand bar also looked up. "Oh, my goodness." Dennis exclaimed as he saw his small motor launch drifting away.

The boating community must be a close fraternity, because another boat owner gestured as he called out, "Come on. We can catch it with my boat." Together, Dennis and the "Good Samaritan" ran to a fair-sized motor launch, boarded quickly, and were soon racing toward the drifting vessel. We all stopped to witness the rescue. Fortunately, the motor launch overtook the smaller boat before it floated into the crashing surf a short distance away. It was then a simple matter for Dennis to secure his boat with a rope. When the two men returned to the sand bar, they were met with cheerful enthusiasm. Shortly after the rescue, the rising tide ended our efforts at collecting our edible treasures. Reluctantly, we climbed aboard Dennis's boat and returned to shore.

At the Stevenson home, we put the still-living clams into a pail of fresh water, where the clams pumped out the salt water along with the sand that is ever-present in a clamshell. It was easy to process the clam meat and to grind the clams into a hamburger consistency for soups and stews. Loaded with a treasure trove of clam meat, we were ready to return to our home in Cottage Grove.

Before we left, Dennis invited, "Perc, why don't we go downtown to an antique store to see what they have in old tools?" Dennis and I shared many common interests, including old tools and used equipment. I felt comfortable with his abbreviation of my name part of the intimacy of a close friendship. "Great!" I replied, "I have been looking for a cheap lathe, but the ones I've found are beyond my budget." Dennis asserted confidently, "I've seen some stationary power tools from time to time. Perhaps we can find something for you." Since Carolyn and Dennis's wife, Carole, enjoyed visiting with each other, I did not hesitate to take Dennis up on his offer.

As we made our way to the downtown area of Coos Bay, I noticed several thrift shops and secondhand stores. In the musty confines of one old building, we discovered a small cache of worn and rusty tools. "Rust does not indicate that a tool is old or antique," I commented to Dennis. "It only means that the item has been neglected and ignored." Dennis smiled, then said in an excited voice, "Hey, Perc! Take a look at this!"

He reached down in a pile of gardening tools and extracted an old Montgomery Ward wood-lathe of unknown age. It had a twenty-four-inch length and a five inch "throw" (the depth from the arbor to the bed of the lathe). The price tag indicated that the lathe was only $25.00. Although the black paint was chipped and replaced by rust, I looked beyond its age and condition and imagined myself turning a candlestick of creative beauty. Unaware of the extent of needed improvements, I concluded that it constituted a bargain. Dennis nodded approvingly. "Of course," he studied the lathe pensively, "you will have to clean the rusty metal, paint the lathe, free the moving parts, find a motor and a drive belt, build a sturdy tool stand, and acquire some lathe chisels. But, as a result of your labors, you would have a working lathe." I felt like Nazredin Hoja of Middle Eastern legend, who declared his good fortune after finding a horseshoe, "All I need is three more horse shoes and a horse!"

In the weeks that followed, I joyfully spent time in the tasks required to transform this rusty old machine into a working wood-lathe. After a session of rust removal and a can of black spray paint, my old lathe looked new, even if it was rather primitive. I built my own simple lathe stand out of scrap two-by-fours and old plywood salvaged from the burn pile of a nearby construction site (with the permission of the builders). The lathe stand was strong and manageable for moving from the garage to the driveway, where it was often used on warm and sunshiny days.

When Tom Douglas heard of my acquisition, he supplied me with a valuable gift. Unable by Oregon law to use, sell or give away old lathe tools whose metal blades were shorter than six inches, he had retained the worn tools in a bin in his office rather than discard them. One Sunday he brought a set of old tools to the church and gave them to me as a loan to be returned within ninety-nine years. I calculated that I would be obligated to return them to the woodshop class no later than 2072 (139 years following my birth). Officially a loan, it was virtually a gift.

I have to admit that the first effort at turning cost me, for a spray of oil from the exposed three-step pulley laid a stripe of black oil up my shirt from waist to collar. When I entered the house with my soiled white dress shirt, Carolyn looked up wordlessly and shook her head in disgust.

My first project was a bulky candlestick for Mother's Day for Carolyn. Because it was too light of a lathe for heavy turnings, I contented myself with smaller projects. The live center was simply fastened to the arbor by a set screw. The arbor itself had a three-step pulley, matching the one on the old salvaged motor. The tailstock housed a simple pointed rod which served as the "dead" center. Even though it was a cheap old lathe, I was proud of it and enjoyed turning small projects. Maxing out the full 24-inch length of the lathe, I turned a beautiful large oak rolling pin from a discarded table leg for my wife. It is still a unique tool used often in our kitchen. Its weight and length makes rolling out dough a simple and precise task.

Over the years, I longed for "the real thing," a lathe with a long bed and a deep bowl-turning capability. Always on the lookout for a "deal," I waited for years before an exciting opportunity arose. Carolyn and I had decided to spend Friday mornings together. We would shop at garage sales and conclude the morning with lunch together. It was a delightful time enjoying each other and, not incidentally, acquiring some bargains in books, furniture, clothing, and tools.

One Friday morning, as Carolyn and I were making the rounds of the local garage sales, we came upon an antique wood lathe, a 1941 Sears-Dunlap 42-inch lathe. It was a quality piece for only $70. It needed to be mounted, but that was readily accomplished by my neighbor and friend, Tom Pearce, who designed and welded a metal stand with handle and wheels so that it could be moved out into the driveway for use.

Two weeks later, the Lord led us to a garage sale where lathe parts were being sold at a price which was almost a give-away. No lathes were in evidence. The owner simply wanted to get rid of the various lathe parts. Tool rests, live and dead centers (now called "drive centers" and "live centers"), bowl plates, and various lathe parts totaling between $400 and $500 were on sale for $20. I purchased them all, realizing later that they were all perfectly compatible with my lathe. It was the Lord's doing that we should discover two separate garage sales that complemented each other. After cleaning and painting the parts to their original color, matching the lathe, I now enjoy a workable antique wood lathe with all its original parts and colors.

Perhaps the two sales just two weeks apart were a coincidence. But having all the lathe accessories match the antique lathe? That is too much of a coincidence. Perhaps a Greater Power provided for my desire. God does do more than simply meet the needs of His children. To me, the words of the Apostle John still ring true. "He that spared not His own son, but delivered Him up for us all, how shall He not with Him also freely give us all things?" (John 10:30)

28

Trip to the Holy Land
November 1998

Ministering in a small church on a low salary had its compensations. Gracious and generous church members, constantly aware of the modest pastoral remuneration as reflected in the church budget, went out of their way to make up for it. Their kindnesses ranged from hospitality to outright gifts of produce from their gardens and trees. Our church treasurer and her husband, owners of a wholesale grocery company which provided service to local food markets and chain grocery stores, extended their buying power to us as their support of their pastoral family. And while Carolyn and I found that we could ill-afford to spend our meager discretionary funds on pleasures such as entertainment or travel, we were not totally deprived.

Each Christmas, the church gave a gift to the pastor and his family. One Christmas, the congregation presented us with season tickets for our whole family to attend the subscription classical concerts at the local university. Another year at Christmas, they presented us with a gift certificate to redeem at a local nursery, where we could buy plants and trees to improve the landscape around our new home. Another time we received tools for home improvement. Each Christmas, our church family expressed its love and encouragement in some creative gift. Sometimes, it was simply an envelope with the results of their "love offering." Were it not for gestures such as these, we would have felt the limitations of our social activities to a much greater degree. Even as we appreciated these gestures of love and support, we could not help but envy the wider fortunes of our colleagues in larger churches who could afford international travel. Their thrilling reports of visiting the Holy Land filled me with longing. I wished that my own preaching and teaching could be enriched by the experience of "walking where Jesus walked."

In the early years of our ministry in Cottage Grove, I had been visited regularly by a representative of an international travel agency, offering me a free trip to Israel if I could muster eight or more people from our church to take the tour at a full price. I would be bestowed with the dubious honor of being the "tour host" with the responsibility of creating the publicity, scheduling the dates with the travel company, securing special insurance, scheduling travel arrangements, and taking general oversight of the group. Overwhelmed as I was in my new church ministry due to a scarcity of workers in the church, I felt that accepting that kind of offer was not practical.

The lowest-priced seven-day tour offered by the travel agency at that time was at least $2,500. Even if our church members were interested in travel tours, we would not be able to find the minimum number who could afford that cost. The logging industry had dwindled due to the negative impact of the political successes of the environmental movement, and as a result, many forest and mill jobs were lost, and several of our members became unemployed. The more fortunate ones found themselves having to watch every penny in order to live from paycheck to paycheck. I correctly concluded that our church members could not afford even the basic tour of the Holy Land much less the longer and more expensive ones. After my fifth refusal over a period of three years, the representative stopped calling on me. Obviously, I was not a viable candidate for leading a group of tourists. And neither was our church a gold mine from which to recruit eight people who could afford to travel.

So it was a natural response that when the offer came to pay for a week-long trip to the Holy Land from an anonymous source within the church, Carolyn and I grew excited. After the constant stress of a very tight budget, the thought of an international trip, no matter how brief, filled us with joyful anticipation. On the surface, the offer was quite generous, a short, all-expenses-paid trip to the Holy Land. The donor was a lady in our church who preferred to remain anonymous, so the offer was made known to us by the church treasurer. We discovered the identity of our would-be benefactress by accident some time later. At the time of the initial offer, we were thrilled at the prospect and expressed our gratitude to the church treasurer who had conveyed the news to us. In a second communication from the source of the offer, the details revealed the conditions attached to it. For seven days (including the two days of travel to and from the Middle East) we would be able to traverse the length and breadth of the State of Israel, visiting sites of biblical importance.

However, our initial excitement waned slightly as we learned more about the leader of the tour, a theologically controversial teacher with a small devoted group of followers. Apparently, he was also a favorite of our mysterious benefactress, even though he held some convictions that were not biblically defensible. His dogmatic and assertive personality did not inspire us to sit under his teaching. Undoubtedly, the tour would be narrated through his own biblical interpretations, which differed profoundly from mine. How could we enjoy such a trip when we could not trust the teacher to be biblically balanced? Sadly, we realized that we could not accept such a trip in good conscience

However, there was still a workable alternative. A slightly more expensive tour would allow us to enjoy not one week but three weeks on a first-class tour of the Holy Land with a competent tour leader, who also happened to be a close friend. As a true Bible scholar and pastoral colleague, he would enrich our tour experience. Not only that, but the tour would encompass visiting surrounding countries where significant biblical events had taken place. Quickly we calculated the difference in cost and realized that if we stretched our budget just a bit, we could pay the difference and gain a far greater value for each extra dollar spent. In addition, we would be part of a high-quality tour, visiting many more sites of biblical importance.

After talking it over, Carolyn and I agreed that it would not be unacceptable if I suggested to the church treasurer that we would like to augment the monies of our generous sponsor and be included in a much more comprehensive Holy Land tour under the leadership of our intimate friend and enthusiast of Bible history. Our counter-offer pointed out that we would be gaining much more value for each dollar spent and that we would still be most grateful to our generous unknown friend. After all, we reasoned, what church member would not want the pastor and his wife to gain even more value and pleasure from such a generous offer?

We were wrong. Less than a week later, we were approached by our church treasurer, whose crestfallen expression was not encouraging. I thought that at worst we were locked into the original offer despite the changes we had suggested. I began, "So she did not agree with our offer?" "Worse than that, the offer has been withdrawn."

I knew only of one woman in the church who was feisty enough to want it her way or not at all. She had already proven her desire to control when she donated a small Conn organ to the church even when we had no organist to play it. Frantically looking for a musician, we discovered one man in the congregation who played it as best he could. The tempo was slow, but it was organ music. However, he fell ill and could not play for several months. The organ fell silent once again with no one to play it. One Sunday the donor of the organ approached me aggressively and announced, "If you don't find someone to play that organ, I'm taking it back and selling it!" As shocking as it was to discover that her gift organ had "strings attached to it," I tried to tactfully encourage her to be patient. "I am sure that Sam (our organist) is getting much better and will be playing the organ again." Inwardly, I was tempted to tell her to take the organ back. The idea of offering conditional gifts to the Lord through his church was offensive and, frankly, dangerous but I controlled my impulse to confront her. She seemed to be the kind of person who would be quick to take offense as her response to a rebuke. While she did not demand that the organ be returned to her at that time, true to her character, she continued to threaten that unless the organ was used, she would confiscate it and sell it.

So it was not difficult to guess the identity of the feisty "benefactress" who withdrew her offer of a gift trip to the Holy Land. Later, when her identity slipped out by accident, we were not surprised. The whole painful experience fit in with her way of doing things. Our aspirations to see the Holy Land faded away as we refocused our attention on our ministry. It was clear that we would not be able to save enough to make the trip on our own for several years, if ever. We finished our ministry in that church several years later without travelling abroad.

However, the Lord had other plans. Evidently, He had not forgotten the height of joy and the depth of disappointment that Carolyn and I had felt when an offer to travel was so suddenly withdrawn.

It was almost eight years later that our friends and tour leaders of trips to the Middle East called on the phone one day, offering to pay my way as a member of their next tour of the Middle East. Dr. Dennis Stevenson's voice boomed out of the receiver as I held it to my ear. "Perc, we are taking an 18-day trip to Greece, Turkey, Jordan and Israel. Would you like to join us? We will pay your way." It was an offer I could not refuse. "Can we take Carolyn along," I asked. "Sure, you will have to pay her way, but we would be glad to have her."

When I informed the church board where I was now serving of the gracious and generous offer, they were enthusiastic and willingly gave me the time off. My father had died a few years earlier, leaving us a modest inheritance. From the inheritance, it was possible for us to pay Carolyn's expenses. This trip was uniquely exciting because it fulfilled a longing generated so many years earlier by the unfortunate withdrawal of a trip to the Holy Land.

We took a second tour to the Middle East two years later and a third, two years after that. Those journeys led us to other international trips on our own. With our missionary daughter and family living in Germany, we travelled to see them, visiting other nations along the way. Our overall count has included six countries of the Middle East, twelve European countries and eight nations of the Pacific Rim.

God more than made up for the aborted Holy Land trip so many years earlier. Although these spectacular trips did not qualify under the category of "needs," we still claim the promise in the Scriptures that our needs (and sometimes desires) are met by our God, the God of all creation. "Delight thyself also in the LORD: and He shall give thee the desires of thine heart. Commit thy way unto the LORD; trust also in Him; and He shall bring it to pass." (Psalm 37:4-5)

29

Flat on I-84
November 2006

The drive from Oregon City to the Wenas Valley north of Yakima, Washington is a truly beautiful trip, especially in the spring, summer and fall seasons of the year. The first 100 miles of freeway going east through the Columbia River Gorge offers a spectacular adventure in natural beauty. Colorful rocky cliffs soar high on the right, their heights covered with evergreen trees in contrast to the bare, multi-hued volcanic faces of the towering cliffs.

Across the shimmering waters of the Columbia, cliffs rise on the Washington State side of the gorge. At the base of the cliffs the yellow cars of the BNSF (Burlington Northern Santa Fe) freight train wind their way from Portland to points east, appearing as small toy electric trains in the distance. Small farms dot the rise of green hillsides above the river gorge. Diminutive towns and isolated communities appear across the river sporadically to the observant automobile occupants.

Glimpses of the rippling river surface can be seen through the branches of the towering deciduous trees lining the shoulder of the interstate highway. A sense of peace descends upon the those observing scenic beauty surrounding them as they approach the towns of Hood River and The Dalles.

Fourteen miles beyond The Dalles lies the tiny community of Biggs Junction, where a dramatic bridge spans the width of the mighty Columbia River, allowing trucks and automobiles travelling north on Highway 395 to enter the state of Washington. In the distance (upriver) is the John Day Dam, one of many controlling the flow of the Columbia River.

Turning north to cross the bridge brings one to the Washington side of the river, up a winding cliff-side road to the top of the northern side of the Columbia Gorge. Looking back from this elevated side of the gorge, one can see the lush wheat fields of Eastern Oregon stretching to the southern horizon. As one passes the attractive community of Goldendale, the road narrows to two lanes as it enters the hills of the Yakima Indian Reservation. The trip through the reservation can be a slow drive, especially when one follows heavily laden trucks carrying goods to and from the Yakima Valley. The boredom of following slow traffic, however, is offset by sixty-two miles of scenic highway through the mountains of the reservation from the Columbia River to the town of Toppenish in the lower Yakima Valley. Going north through town, the road intersects Washington State Highway I-82 running from the Southeast to the Northwest, reaching from the Tri-cities area all the way to Yakima.

Forty miles west, the freeway from Toppenish leads north through the dramatic break in the mountains aptly named Union Gap. Swinging in a westward arc around the city of Yakima, the freeway becomes a highway again as it moves west and then north again through the Naches River Valley. Just before the little community of Naches, 14 miles from Yakima, a turnoff ascends a steep mountain grade up to the Wenas Valley. Although the trip is long and arduous, the scenic rivers and mountains allow the hours to slip away almost unnoticed.

Our trip was to be a vacation of a few days with Carolyn's sister and brother-in-law, who lived in a large, spacious home overlooking the Wenas Valley northwest of Yakima. The spectacular one-hundred-eighty-degree vista from their home included a view of the upper Wenas Valley surrounded by gently rolling mountains. Picturesque farmhouses and country homes surrounded by fields of green, yellow and brown, and pastures dotted with cattle, lent a spirit of tranquility to the valley. The two-hundred-twenty-mile drive from our house to their home would take almost five hours, including a lunch break in The Dalles.

On the day of our trip, we did not begin our journey until 3:00 in the afternoon. Although it was a late start, we felt confident that we could arrive in Yakima by 8:00 or 8:30 in the evening. So, with confidence we set out with our adult son, Mark, anticipating an uneventful journey. Our automobile was heavily packed as we settled in for the rigors of a long trip on a hot afternoon.

Everything was going smoothly until 5:00 p.m. Traversing an isolated stretch of the freeway in the Columbia River Gorge, we felt a sudden vibration in the car. Pulling over swiftly to the shoulder of the road, we discovered a large bulge in the sidewall of our left rear tire. Since the spare tire and the jack were under the trunk space, we were compelled to unload all the luggage and the other gear we were bringing to our hosts in order to access the spare. With the primitive jack and inadequate ratchet, we struggled to remove the faulty tire, but to no avail. I began to have visions of an expensive tow to the next city and wondered how long it would take an AAA tow truck to arrive. Hood River was already behind us. The next offramp was at least seven miles ahead of us in the tiny community of Mosier. It was 26 miles to The Dalles. No tow truck could possibly arrive in time to allow us to continue our journey this day. The prospects for road assistance looked grim.

After a half hour of Mark's persistent effort, we finally removed the flat tire. However, to our consternation, we discovered that the spare was one of those undersized wheels which could not support the weight of our load for the long trip ahead. Nevertheless, we mounted it in the place of the damaged tire. However, it was clear that for us to continue our journey, we would have to purchase a new tire. The small spare was not recommended for either high speed travel or for automotive stability while driving. The only option was for us to purchase a new tire. But the nearest tire company, Les Schwab, was ahead of us in The Dalles.

A ubiquitous tire chain in the State of Oregon, Les Schwab began in the central Oregon city of Bend. It was widely known for its quality products along with its swift and courteous service to its customers.

Glancing at our watches, we realized that it was now 5:30 p.m., and the Les Schwab Tire Company usually closed at 6:00 p.m. We would never be able to drive the 26 miles to The Dalles at a lower speed, locate the store in the city, and still arrive during business hours. I weighed the risks of driving at a high speed on an inadequate spare and rejected the idea out of hand. It was clear that we could not arrive in The Dalles in time to purchase a new tire.

Since our trip schedule was now unalterably changed, my fears now included not only the expense of a new tire but the costs of overnight lodging and meals as well. Somehow, we would have to communicate to Carolyn's sister that we would not be arriving until the next day. Added to that, the responsibility for the welfare and comfort of my wife and son weighed heavily upon me.

Praying inwardly for help, I looked up as my wife suggested, "Why don't we call Suzanne in Portland and ask her to contact the Les Schwab tire store in Oregon City? She could explain our predicament and ask them to contact the store in The Dalles. If someone there would be willing to stay late after the business normally closed, we might be able to purchase a new tire and continue on our trip." It was a great idea. Fortunately, we were in cell phone range of some unseen tower. After placing the call, we silently prayed as we waited for Suzanne's return call. Precious minutes flitted by. To our relief, the phone rang, but it was already 5:45, probably too late to find the tire store open. According to our calculations, it would take about 25 to 30 minutes for us to arrive in The Dalles.

"Hi, Dad" Suzanne's voice was upbeat, a sign that good news was on its way. "I called the Les Schwab store here, and the people have been really understanding. They contacted the store in The Dalles, and told them about you. The folks in The Dalles will wait for you, and they said not to hurry. They will be there when you arrive." "Really!" I replied. "That is incredible. We'll get on the road right away." Suzanne cautioned, "Don't hurry. The folks here at our Les Schwab want you to be safe. They are really nice people!"

After terminating the call, we repacked our luggage and possessions into our little 1989 Mercury Tracer and carefully proceeded to The Dalles. By the time we arrived, it was close to 6:30 p.m., long past closing time. As we pulled in to the service area, three men ran out to greet us before we could exit from the car. "Thanks for waiting for us," I began. "It is very kind of you." The leader of the crew replied, "We are glad to help. Let's see what we can do for you." Recognizing our hot and exhausted condition, they escorted us into the now deserted, air-conditioned store and swiftly mounted a pair of tires to replace the worn and damaged ones on the rear wheels of the automobile. It was not a mere sales ploy. "It's best to replace a pair of tires to keep the ride balanced. We'll place the new ones on the rear to keep traction positive," the store manager explained. "That way, you will have a safe and comfortable trip."

Treating us as if we were their most treasured and wealthy customers, they invited us to rest at one of their tables. Offering us a cold carbonated drink and a bag of popcorn, they quickly replaced our worn tires, and shortly thereafter announced that we were "ready to go."

I was aware that it might have been possible for this crew to require a surcharge for the inconvenience of having to stay late to help us. Not so. They made it seem as if we were doing them a favor by shopping there when indeed we were the ones indebted to them. They had waited for us when they could have been home enjoying their families. Offering us whatever refreshments they had on hand, they saw to our comfort as best as they could. Brushing aside our thanks, they wished us well on our trip and waved as we pulled out of the service stall to continue our journey. "We called our wives and told them to hold up dinner for us, so it's no real sacrifice for us to work a little late. In fact, you're not the first. We have done this many times." The parting words of the store manager lingered in my ears.

We safely arrived at our destination just a little later than originally scheduled, strongly aware of God's hand in our affairs. After all, the truth of Scripture is unbreakable. "God is our refuge and strength, an ever-present help in trouble. Therefore, we will not fear..." (Psalm 46:1-2)

30

Incident at Lake Geneva
January 2007

The anticipation of seeing family at the end of our trip made the 11-hour Luftansa Airline flight from Portland, Oregon to Frankfurt, Germany a little more bearable. While the great circle flight taxed the endurance of the two-hundred-twenty passengers crowded aboard the Airbus 320, the flight attendants did all they could to aid our comfort. Despite the crowded conditions, which made our travel a little uncomfortable, Carolyn and I were so eagerly anticipating our three-week visit in Germany with our daughter and son-in-law that we ignored the inconvenience of the small seats and narrow aisles of the plane. Passengers constantly traversed the aisles to and from the much-used restroom facilities. The babble of loud conversations in German, French and English, and the occasional crying of little children, did little to dampen our enthusiasm. We were going to see our grandchildren! Even though I was suffering pain from my left hip, due to a twenty-five-year-old injury suffered in an automobile accident, I managed to be mobile enough with the aid of crutches.

The sun set in the west and rose again in the east before our flight landed at the huge Frankfurt airport. We taxied to a stop in a line of airliners parked two miles from the main terminal. Buses awaited us, and after informally loading passengers and carry-on luggage, they transported us to the customs branch of the terminal. With our passports boasting a visa stamp, we entered the terminal to await the next leg of our trip. After a short layover, a second flight of less than two hours landed us in the Basel/Mulhouse Airport near the city of Basel, Switzerland, only a half hour drive from the village of Kandern, Germany, where our daughter and her husband were missionaries and where our two granddaughters attended the Black Forest Academy. The Basel/Mulhouse International Airport straddled the border of France and Switzerland, which border ran down the middle of the main terminal. Exiting from the wrong doors would lead to confusion, complications and expense, but having been warned to exit the terminal from the Swiss side, we were met by our family with warm hugs and kisses.

We were especially anxious to see our young granddaughters again. They impressed us with their growing maturity which only served to emphasize that we had missed many phases of their lives due to the separation of time and distance. While Carolyn and I wished to spend as much time as we could with our family, we knew that our three-week visit would also afford us the opportunity of making day-trips to nearby places of interest. Since Kandern is situated less than a half hour from the borders of Switzerland and France, the options for travel were numerous.

In preparation for travelling on the SBB (Schweizerische Bundesbahnen) the Swiss national train system known for its punctuality and comfort, we had anticipated obtaining ten-day Eurail passes, which allowed us to travel anywhere. But we learned that they were very expensive, and that a local ticket in Switzerland would cost much less. Even though we were soon armed with specific tickets to Lausanne, Switzerland, the multiple tracks crisscrossing each other, with several trains making use of the same tracks, made the schedule a complicated booklet of times and destinations. Train numbers, times of arrival and departure, bus and streetcar schedules, all served to confuse us. However, they made perfect sense to the Swiss, who formed the bulk of the passengers aboard the train.

As our first venture into Switzerland, we chose to visit the Chateau de Chillon, a medieval castle located on the east end of Lake Geneva, a banana-shaped body of water curving north and to the east. At the bottom of the banana-shaped lake was the Swiss capitol city of Geneva. At the top of the lake was the city of Lausanne. To the east of Lausanne was the target of our journey.

The trip could be accomplished in a single day but would require rising early in the morning and arriving home late in the darkness of night. However, the attraction of taking an exciting trip in a foreign country on our own, without a guide, to a beautiful destination of historical and religious significance excited us. So after acclimating ourselves at the home of our "German" branch of the family for a few days, we packed lightly for the trip south.

Prepared with a single backpack holding our necessities and snacks, we were driven early the next morning through the Swiss/German border and into the beautiful city of Basel. Quaint streetcars moved along tracks in the center of the streets as small European automobiles navigated their way through the narrow traffic lanes and the wider boulevards. Ever vigilant for our welfare, our daughter, Catherine, escorted us into the cavernous SBB train station while David, her husband, parked the car in the station parking garage and hurried to meet us at the ticket counter. While we waited in line, I had an opportunity to take in the immensity of the station.

The main room was huge. Whereas crowds of people stood in lines at ticket counters, entering and exiting from restroom facilities and eating at various snack counters, others moved decisively toward the large, wide stairs leading to the departure platforms. Yet it was all strangely orderly. With two large banks of stairs, travelers were ascending on the right and descending on the left. A fleeting thought reminded me of Grand Central Station in New York City. With one exception. While this crowd was mainly Swiss, it included a large variety of internationals. Perhaps this was because the city of Basel is an international city, located on the border of three countries Germany, France and Switzerland. By train it was not far from other cultures in Italy, Lichtenstein, Austria and destinations beyond.

On this day, our trip would take us from Basel south, through quaint towns and villages dotting incredibly beautiful countryside, with the ever-present backdrop of the Swiss Alps. Our destination was Lausanne, 204 km (126.8 miles) south of Basel. From there we would take a local commuter train east 29.7 km (18.4 miles) to Montreux. Another 9 miles by bus would bring us to Veytaux. A half-mile walk further east would end our travel at the ramparts of the Chateau de Chillon. It was a simple enough trip. But the excitement of travel in one of the most beautiful areas of the world kept us gawking like tourists, which we were. The first-class rail cars were spacious and comfortable, large windows accommodating us to a view of unparalleled beauty.

By mid-morning, we found ourselves in Montreux. Two more easy steps of transportation by train and bus found us in Veytaux with Chateau de Chillon in sight. Behind the towers of the castle rose the snow-capped peaks of the Italian Alps. We were on the southern border of Switzerland. Accustomed to the crutches by now, I had no trouble covering the relatively short distance to the bridge that gapped the space between the shore and the rocky island upon which the castle had been built.

Our selection of the Chateau de Chillon was not an accidental happenstance of random tourism. From the eleventh century (1005 AD) the buildings on the island had begun to take form, developing into a fully functional castle guarding the main trade route through the alpine Great St. Bernard Pass connecting Switzerland and Italy. However, it was not until the sixteenth century that a drama of historical dimensions took place.

A Genovese monk, Prior of the monastery of St. Victor in Geneva, was arrested in 1530 by the Dukes of Savoy for refusing to abandon his new-found faith as articulated in the biblical tenets of the Protestant Reformation. After two years of imprisonment, he was transferred to the dungeon at Chateau de Chillon, where he languished for over four more years, chained to a rock pillar in the cold and damp atmosphere of the dark dungeon. Lord Byron, the renowned English poet, visited the site centuries later and was so moved by the story of Francois de Bonivard that he wrote the famous poem, *The Prisoner of Chillon*.

While many other prisoners (his two brothers included) died from starvation, torture, and exposure to the damp and cold conditions, somehow Francois de Bonivard survived. All the while, Francois determinedly refused to recant his faith in the Lord. His imprisonment ended after years of incarceration and torture when the castle fell in battle to more friendly Reformation forces.

Over time, this castle on the northern shore of Lake Geneva, at the very eastern tip, became a symbol both of horrific torture and towering faith. This was our destination as suggested to us by my well-travelled brother, Charles.

The castle itself, was incredibly fascinating. Restored in the late 19th century, it still retained evidence of its former glory. Inside the castle were fearsome weapons, extravagant furniture and stunningly beautiful architectural designs enhanced by spectacular wood carvings, striking painting and geometric tile work. In its glory days, the castle must have been a showcase of splendor. It was difficult for me to imagine the gaiety of the castle inhabitants while others suffered pain and death below in the dungeon.

Just above the level of the lake, the dungeon certainly created a different impression. Large open archways looked out on the lake. Escape was not a possibility since the prisoners were chained to the pillars and rocks. The sewage of the castle flowed into the lake just outside the large openings, the stench becoming an invisible wall. Cold and dampness permeated the dungeon, especially in the frozen winter months. There was no protection against the elements. Even the modern tourist could easily envision that this was a place of pain, discomfort and death.

With some surprise, I found myself able to traverse the rough ground, the rickety stairs and the short ladders of the castle. I was even able to keep my balance on the narrow catwalks of the castle's defense system.

Soon our self-guided tour was over, and it was time to return to Basel, where our daughter and son-in-law awaited our train's arrival.

Tired, we caught a local bus from the castle to the town of Montreux, arriving a bit early for the commuter train to Lausanne. When it arrived headed in the direction of Lausanne, I suggested that Carolyn and I could wait for our train north more comfortably in the Lausanne train station than the primitive platform in Montreux, for the Lausanne train station afforded more comfortable seats in the waiting area. Over her hesitation, I insisted, so, we boarded the commuter train heading in the general direction of Lausanne. It proved to be a disastrous decision.

Our first local stop was at St. Sulpice. No problem there. I reasoned that it was one of the local stops between Montreux and Lausanne. Even though the stops at Preverenges and Morge' were unfamiliar, I assuaged my growing uncertainty with the thought that Lausanne was just ahead. Little did I know at the time that we had long since bypassed Lausanne. My anxiety rose as it began to dawn on me that we were no longer headed west but had turned south. And it was getting dark. We had been on the train much longer than it had taken us when we travelled earlier in the day from Lausanne to Montreux. With no map to consult, we had no idea of where we were at any of the stops along the route.

Carolyn grew increasingly disturbed, insisting that we were on the wrong train and headed in a direction which was taking us further away from Basel by the moment. Obviously, we had missed our stop in Lausanne. Realizing my mistake, I became a little more uncertain and disturbed at my own stupidity. Indeed, we were headed down the west side of Lake Geneva toward the capitol of Switzerland. More time passed as the train stopped at small stations in towns and villages. After Etoy and Perroy, the train came to a stop in Rolle. We were halfway down the west side of Lake Geneva on our way to Geneva when Carolyn insisted that we step out of the train. Our hosts, David and Catherine, would be awaiting us in Basel, and we had already missed the train from Lausanne. It was a certainty that we would be late in arriving in Basel because we now had much more distance to cover on our trip home.

At Rolle, with a sudden sense of urgency, we left the train car and quickly stepped through the closing doors out onto the platform. The platform was elevated to the height of the train cars so that it was possible to step into or out of a train car without effort. As our train departed, I felt the insecurity of being lost in a foreign country without adequate knowledge regarding the Swiss train schedule. The only consolation was that we had our passports for identification and a few Euros to meet any incidental expenses.

As we glanced about us, we noticed a large backlit sign with train numbers, symbols, times of arrival and departure, and destinations near and far. Although written in English, the schedule was confusing to us. Unfamiliar symbols and cryptic abbreviations kept us from a clear understanding of the intent of their meaning. Studying the complicated train schedule, we began to feel the panic of not being able to cope. The tide of passengers who had just left the same commuter train we had vacated swept their way toward the ascending staircase to the overhead walkway leading to the main building of the Rolle train station. Watching them for a moment, we realized that it would take us another half hour to enter the train terminal, stand in line, and finally secure the correct information leading us to the right platform. By then, we might miss an appropriate train, necessitating an even longer wait for the next one. Our indecision must have communicated itself to passers-by.

As we discussed what to do next, a young man stopped beside us. He was carrying a backpack and was dressed in casual clothes. Pleasantly, in accented English, he asked, "May I be of help to you?" Gratefully we responded, "Yes." I added an explanation. "We are confused by the schedule. We hoped to be on our way to Basel, but we took the wrong train. We need to get back to Basel. Our children are waiting for us. We will be late as it is." Pausing, I added, "Are you familiar with the schedule?" "Yes, I live here," he responded.

Studying the schedule for a moment, the young man said, "You are on the right platform. The train you are hoping to take stops here. It will be the next train." Looking down the long platform, he added with some surprise, "As a matter of fact, here it comes right now. When it stops, get aboard. It will take you quickly to Basel. It is an express."

At that moment a train engine pulling a long line of cars raced by the platform, braking to a stop a few seconds later. As the doors of the train hissed open, the young man assisted us in boarding the first-class car that had stopped before us. Then smiling, he bade us farewell. As we thanked him, he turned and made his way down the platform toward the steps leading to the main train station. Relieved, we settled into our seats, all-the-while thanking God for the unexpected assistance of a stranger. Soon our train accelerated into the night, leaving the lights of the station far behind. We were on our way home.

True to the young man's prediction, our express train arrived in Basel ahead of the one which we had originally hoped to board in Lausanne for the return ride.

Later, as we pondered our experience, we concluded that it had to be of the Lord that we stepped off the train in Rolle rather than at some earlier train stop.

It had to be of the Lord that a young man whom we had never met before should step out of the crowd of passengers rushing along the platform toward the main station, to help us.

It had to be of the Lord that the express train from Geneva to Basel arrived at the Rolle platform just at that moment.

It had to be of the Lord that our express train arrived at our destination in Basel earlier than the one we had originally planned to board.

And, it had to be of the Lord that we had an experience to share with David and Catherine that once again illustrated God's loving care for His children, even in the smallest details of a wrong decision, a confusing train schedule, the assistance of a complete stranger, and an express train ride home.

"Fear thou not; for I am with thee: be not dismayed; for I am thy God: I will strengthen thee; yea, I will help thee; yea, I will uphold thee with the right hand of My righteousness." (Isaiah 41:10)

31

At God's Expense
Winter 2007

The history of our house improvements over the years has been a litany of God's benevolence upon our family. A year after arriving in Oregon City to serve at the Victory Baptist Church, we began to plan for the purchase of a house.

For the first year of our ministry, the future of the church was in doubt. An acrimonious church split before we arrived and a power struggle between two factions in the church upon our arrival indicated that a positive prognosis for the health of the congregation was by no means certain. Consequently, we did not feel that it was a good idea to commit ourselves to the immediate purchase of a home but rather to rent a house until a more positive future was certain.

A gracious gesture from one of the member families of the church, made their rental house available to us at a very reasonable rate. However, after a year of ministry, we felt confident enough to risk purchasing a home of our own. Unfortunately, our eligibility for a home loan was in question, not because of our credit rating (which was the highest), or because of our modest wages, but because of the size of our family (three adolescent children). However, as we applied for a Veterans Administration loan, the loan officer viewed our marginal economic situation against our perfect credit score and approved the loan at his discretion.

After living in the house for a year, we were financially able to add a master bedroom and an attached bathroom, using the capital gains from the sale of our house in Cottage Grove. Much of the labor for this addition was freely supplied by a team of church members. It resulted in a home large enough to welcome grown children and grandchildren when the opportunity presented itself.

When the house needed painting, a team of church members descended upon our home, armed with brushes, ladders, modest scaffolding, and joyful, willing spirits to paint simply for the cost of the supplies. Later, reroofing of the house was done by two members, Phil and Brian, who specialized in that skill, again simply for the cost of the material.

After a few years of occupancy, we extended the living room, adding a large bay window to the front of the house. Our friend, Donny Vitro, lent his expertise and volunteer labor to build the addition for us.

Because the extended living room and bay window now covered the small cement walkway from the driveway to the front door, we were faced with the necessity of a new walkway. This was designed by one of our deacons, assisted by a team of church members. Highly discounted materials kept our costs down.

When our front door succumbed to water damage during a violent rain storm 20 years later, a used door was purchased at a recycling firm for $10. Our friend, Brian, refinished it beautifully. Some time earlier, an old 13½ inch by 19½ inch stained-glass window lay in pieces in a "free" box at a neighborhood garage sale. I had picked it up and brought it home with the idea of someday repairing it as a decorative piece. For seven years, it had lain in a box in the garage, carefully padded against further accidental damage. When an artist in stained-glass began attending our church, she volunteered to repair the broken stained-glass window. Without cost, she replaced the cracked and broken pieces and restored the window to its former glory. This window now graces our front door, adding beauty and light to our living room.

There are a few days of unbearable heat in Oregon City each year. When our water heater expired due to use and age, one of the men from the church, our friend Lud Carlson, installed the newer model which we had purchased, not charging us for his expertise or labor. He also installed a new furnace complete with cooling coils in anticipation of a future air conditioning unit.

Some years after the furnace was replaced in our home, a couple of gifted people joined our church. Dan and Diane Collins took leadership to complete the building project of the church far beyond the modest original plans. Their leadership not only included construction and dealing with the exigencies of bureaucracy but also consisted of their personal purchase of two large classroom units which now complete the church complex as the office building and the youth center. One warm day, Dan and Lud showed up at our home with a large central air conditioning system, which they installed that same day. When I offered to pay for unit, they responded, "The Company bought it." Later, I realized the significance of this statement. Dan was the owner of the company, and to all intents and purposes, he was "The Company!" He had purchased the unit and installed it on our property at his own expense, refusing to take any credit for his generosity.

The provision of the Lord did not end there. But even up to that point, the Hand of the Lord was obvious. While we were not always conscious of God's meeting our needs, His gifts and supply for our needs was regular and constant. As if underlining the biblical truth, God's direct support was simply emphasizing His promise to the Apostle Paul so long ago. "But my God shall supply all your need according to His riches in glory by Christ Jesus." (Philippians 4:19)

32

Kitchen Remodel
Summer 2008

It was not an expensive house. Comfortable? Yes. Well-built? Not really. The floors were carpeted over bare plywood. There was no underlayment. The single-paned windows did little to shut out the cold. The three-bedroom single bath house was obviously a tract home built as cheaply and inexpensively as possible. The drafty, smoke-stained fireplace leaked smoke into the front room. The brick façade was stained with smoke. Situated on a lot with an undefined boundary on one side, the house was built when lax zoning laws were not enforced complicating the legitimate boundaries of the property. We had now lived in our house for twenty-two years. During that time, we had made a few necessary improvements. For instance, a newly designed deck adjacent to our new sliding glass doors in the family room did much to improve the quality of living in our home.

The major problem had proved to be the kitchen. Poorly designed, it did not allow for more than one person at a time to function in the kitchen space. The angled design of the counter did not permit the refrigerator door to open fully. The narrow cabinets barely accommodated the width of a dinner plate, and the shallow drawers could not hold our silverware. Consequently, we were hard-pressed to find adequate storage for the kitchenware necessary for food preparation. As if that were not enough, the cabinets and drawers were constructed of the cheapest fiberboard covered with a thin veneer whose finish had long since worn off. To add insult to injury, years of exposure to moisture had swelled the fiberboard drawer joints. No longer did the faces of the drawers remain attached. The formica countertops were worn and in some places cracked.

So, it was not a surprise when Carolyn suggested rather strongly that we needed to remodel our kitchen. "Our cabinets and drawers are falling apart (indeed, they were disintegrating with every usage), and they need to be replaced." Carolyn clarified her vision. "I don't want a huge, expensive project. Simply replacing the cabinets would satisfy me." With that thought in mind, we determined to spend the money, a somewhat expensive project on replacing the cabinets and drawers as well as resurfacing the countertops with new formica. After some frank discussion about our finances, we concluded that although the cost would probably be prohibitive, we were compelled to take on the task.

God had other plans.

Attending our church were our exceptional friends, Dan and Diane Collins. They had joined the membership a few years earlier and had volunteered, almost immediately, to take charge of our church's building project. We had first met them when I had presided at the wedding ceremony of their daughter and soon-to-be son-in-law. A year later Dan and Diane had visited our church and become members. Skilled in the building trades, they were the owners of an industrial heating, ventilation and air conditioning company. Familiar with the heavy construction projects of factories, schools and high-rise buildings, they were uniquely fitted to supervise our church's modest building program.

When Diane learned of our plans to replace kitchen cabinets, she eagerly offered her services. She was proficient in industrial drafting and offered to draw plans for our new kitchen. We were shocked when she arrived a few days later with a plan for the complete renovation of the space. "You will have to knock out the pantries, remove all cabinets and countertops, strip the walls bare (down to the studs), and remove the ceiling with its insulation," she cheerfully announced. Then, providing a set of drawings, she frankly asked, "What is your budget? How much do you intend to spend for the cabinets?" We told her that the cabinets alone from Home Depot would cost around $14,000, not to mention replacing the counter tops with formica. Of course, we would still be limited by the original design of the kitchen, which allowed for only one person to work in the space without being crowded. Smiling, she announced, "A total renovation such as I have designed would only cost you about $20,000, and you will get so much more for your money if we can recruit volunteers from the church." Then she displayed her beautiful plans for the space which once contained our old kitchen. Totally redesigned, our new kitchen would include rearrangement of the appliances, making room for 2 to 4 people to work at the same time in the open space.

Acting as our contractor, Diane called in every favor she could to accomplish her design. Several men from the church helped us with the demolition of our kitchen. One of the young men, Nick LaVoie, spent hours demolishing the ceiling amid a shower of falling fluffs of fiberglass insulation. Even wearing a mask to protect his lungs from the fine fiberglass dust, he found it a very uncomfortable task. Yet this good-natured young man cheerfully completed the work.

Soon all that was left of our kitchen were the stud walls and bare floor. Plastic sheets stapled to wall studs and ceiling rafters, replaced the spaces where the sheetrock had been removed, insuring a slower loss of heat from the rest of the house. Lud rewired the entire room with outlets and under-the-cabinet lighting. Another friend re-routed the plumbing. Still another of Diane's friends brought his team and expertly affixed new sheetrock to the studs. A second electrician from our church updated our old, inadequate electrical panel. A professional installer, another friend of Diane, laid down a beautiful floor.

Before long before the custom cabinet makers installed the beautiful oak cabinets created in their shop. Their precision wood counters only awaited granite tiles to complete a gorgeous renovation. It was beyond our original dreams to receive quality, custom-made cabinets for the same amount that Home Depot would have charged for a much lesser quality product.

Diane herself installed granite tiles on the bare wooden counter. The effect of the finished project was stunning. The new kitchen boasted twice the storage space as the old one. Best of all, several people could work together in the redesigned space, even though it all fit into the original square footage. Some of the professional workers charged for their labor and materials, but the cost was ridiculously low. Others donated their labor.

At the completion party to which all the workers were invited, we calculated that the kitchen remodeling project costs remained within the estimated budget of $20,000. However, the result was a kitchen that would have cost three times that much. A $50,000 to $60,000 kitchen for only $20,000? It was the gracious provision of the Lord. Once again, we were overwhelmed by God's doing more than we could ever imagine. "Now unto Him that is able to do exceeding abundantly above all that we ask or think, according to the power that worketh in us, unto Him *be* glory in the church by Christ Jesus throughout all ages, world without end. Amen." (Ephesians 3:20-21)

33

"We Will Not Fear"
August 2009

The diagnosis was serious. My neurologist, a young woman who normally had a positive outlook and a ready smile, looked at me seriously and informed me that an MRI had confirmed that there was a cyst in my spinal column pressing against my spinal cord. I had been suffering from excruciating shooting pains down the outer side of my left leg for several months, pain that is usually caused by a pinching of the sciatic nerve somewhere in the spinal column. The MRI (Magnetic Resonance Imaging) had confirmed it.

The neurologist was so youthful in appearance that I simply had to ask about her experience as a physician. She smiled and said, "I don't mind your asking. I was a U.S. Army surgeon for two years in Iraq, operating on our wounded soldiers who had severe neurological damage due to wounds suffered in combat." Then she added enthusiastically, "I know just what to do to help you. I can take out that cyst on your spine and enable you to recover. Of course, sometimes these situations resolve themselves without surgery. We don't know why, but it happens now and then. We can schedule your surgery for a week from now." Then she explained that the necessary surgery carried increased risks: continued pain, a possible stroke, or even (in my case) a fatal heart attack during surgery. Even in her dire warnings, I warmed to this competent surgeon in the body and person of a cheerful young lady. She exuded competence and inspired confidence.

After I arrived home, I tried to maintain a calm exterior, but inwardly I was fearful. Unanswered questions plagued my mind. *Could my heart take the strain of anesthesia and surgery?* Or even worse, *would I suffer a stroke and be a vegetable all the rest of my life? How would my beloved wife cope with my disability? Would I live to see my grandchildren again? Would the expenses of surgery and recovery drain our savings and overtax our already tight budget?* We were on a limited income as retirees.

Guilt also sat heavily upon me. *Why was I torturing myself with these fears? Shouldn't I be an example of faith and trust in the Lord?* No matter my outward confidence, inwardly I had to admit to myself that I was afraid. Even though anxiety was a natural part of this kind of stress, I kept asking myself, *will the surgery be a success, or will I now face the end of a useful life?* Thankful for having enrolled in the Navigators Topical Memory System as a teenager, I began to recall some of the verses from the Bible that I had learned so long ago. Philippians 4:6-7 came to mind, and as I repeated it to myself, I found my anxiety subsiding.

"Be anxious for nothing, but in everything by prayer and supplication with thanksgiving let your requests be made known to God. And the peace of God, which surpasses all comprehension, will guard your hearts and your minds in Christ Jesus." Philippians 4:6-7 (NASB)

Yet, fear still lurked in the back of my mind. *What if I should die?* All the questions related to that event arose in my mind. *How would my wife cope? Did my retirement provide adequately for her financial security all the remaining days of her life? Should I die, who knew me well enough to preside over my funeral? Could my wife and family find the relevant documents and necessary papers needed to resolve the estate? How would my young granddaughters deal with the death of their beloved grandpa?* As I fretted, the words of Psalm 46:1-3 comforted me.

"God is our refuge and strength, an ever-present help in trouble. Therefore, we will not fear, though the earth give way and the mountains fall into the heart of the sea, though its waters roar and foam and the mountains quake with their surging." (Psalm 46:1-3 NIV)

Still, loneliness ate at me as I lay awake in the middle of the night. *What would my existence be like if I suffered a totally debilitating stroke? After all, no one could help me if the worst occurred. Carolyn could not lift me should my condition require it. My home was not adapted to the needs of a stroke victim.* Further, I did not relish the possibility of spending the rest of my life abandoned in a nursing home with only occasional visits from my wife and children. *Who would come and visit me if I could not respond to them?* As I struggled with the issue of loneliness, Psalm 34:4 came to mind, and a peaceful hope overtook resignation in my heart once again.

"I sought the Lord, and he heard me, and delivered me from all my fears." (Psalm 34:4)

Finally, the scheduled day arrived. Early in the morning I checked in to the hospital for surgery. After I was admitted to the surgical ward, the attending nurses prepped me for the scheduled operation, shaving my back and marking the location of the critical vertebrae with a washable marking pencil. They established an intravenous tube into my arm with numerous ports for the injection of various medications. My calm and cheerful wife stayed with me as the pre-surgery preparations took place. Our pastor, Mike, came to pray with us, remaining to visit for a brief time. The anesthesiologist arrived and interviewed me regarding allergies, informing me of the various types of anesthesia I would be receiving and reviewing recovery room procedures. He noted that along with the anesthesia, a drug would be administered that would erase short-term memory so that I would not remember the discomfort of the recovery room. A phlebotomist arrived and took blood samples for typing and lab examination. The physician's assistant brought a pre-surgery check list to be completed. I was given two small pills to relax me prior to being wheeled into the operating room. It had been a long wait, but the pills began to take effect, and any lingering anxiety disappeared.

After a long delay, the neurosurgeon entered the room. She was dressed in a fresh surgical green uniform. "How are you?" she cheerfully inquired. "Are you feeling any pain?"

"No," I answered. "For the past four or five days, the pain has abated somewhat. I feel fairly pain-free." Taken aback, she thought for a moment. Then to make sure, she repeated, "So you are not in pain now?" "No," I answered, adding, "But the folks at the church have been praying for me, and perhaps their prayers are the reason I feel much better." "Could be," she admitted. "I've seen it before." After a moment she decisively concluded, "Then we should not do the surgery. Perhaps the cyst has shrunk. You know, it does sometimes. Why subject you to surgery if it is possible for the pain to permanently disappear? It has happened to six patients of mine. Perhaps it will be true of you. We will not operate today. And we will monitor you for the next two weeks. If the pain returns, we can always do another MRI and schedule surgery. But it may not be necessary at all."

Two weeks later I was still pain-free. The following Sunday, I stood in church and thanked the Lord for the prayers of His people and for His gracious answer to prayer. I realized in the following weeks that sometimes we fear that which may never take place.

But my eldest daughter put the focus into perspective just before I checked into the hospital, saying, "Dad, I love Joshua 1:9. You ought to read it." It read:

"Have not I commanded thee? Be strong and of a good courage; be not afraid, neither be thou dismayed: for the LORD thy God *is* with thee whithersoever thou goest." (Joshua 1:9)

34

The Front Door
March 2010

Our house had been dark for many years. The way it was built accounted for much of its darkness. With its front facing north and with its small windows, it was not bright and airy inside. Even during the day, the interior lights needed to be on. Otherwise, the atmosphere within tended to be depressing. An effort on our part to alleviate this problem yielded some improvement, yet the basic problem remained. In a part of the country (Oregon) where skies were overcast much of the year, there simply was not enough sunlight to lend a cheery and bright atmosphere through the windows. The multitude of glowing table and floor lamps only served as a reminder that nighttime was rapidly approaching.

Partly to relieve this situation, we engaged in a renovation project. An extension of the living room by 3 feet along with the addition of a bay window (with three large windows) increased the light in the room. Still, it was darker than desired. A solar tube, judicially placed in the ceiling at the darkest half of the room, did improve the atmosphere considerably. Even with all the renovation, the darkest corner of the living room was at the front door. Somehow the shadows concentrated there, much to our disappointment. However, out of adversity God provided for that need as well.

The provision for light in our living room had begun years before. One bright Friday morning Carolyn and I began to visit some neighborhood garage sales as part of our Friday morning "together time." We arose earlier than usual, ate a quick breakfast and left the house to make the usual round of garage and yard sales. By noon, we satisfied our hunger at a local eatery. This became a pattern for our Friday mornings. The variety of cast-off items caught our interest, but frugality was the rule of the day. Many Friday mornings we would purchase nothing, simply satisfying our interest in the diversity of "treasures" being sold at bargain prices.

One morning, while meandering between tables laden with items now being offered for a fraction of their original purchase price, we noticed a cardboard box at the foot of the driveway with the word "Freebies" printed in black letters from a Sharpie marker on the side of the box. Wandering over to the box, I noticed among other items of uncollectable junk the remains of a leaded glass window. Loose pieces pulled away from the "lead came" (the "H" shaped lengths of lead that bind the glass pieces together). Collecting the pieces of the stained-glass window, I inquired of the homeowners as to its origin. They informed me that it had come from the remains of an old German Pentecostal church which had burned down in Portland during the early 1930's. Someone in their family had collected the pieces with the hope of repairing and restoring the window to its former beauty. But as the years passed, it had lain in the darkness of their garage only to be discovered by these present homeowners with whom I was speaking.

History had repeated itself, and the glass pieces and twisted "lead came" rested again in the darkness of their garage for many years. Finally deciding that nothing could be done to repair the stained-glass window, the "garage sale" homeowners simply put it in the "freebie" box, hoping that someone would take the pieces and hopefully restore them to their original beauty.

History repeated itself again as the pieces of the once beautiful window rested safely between protective insulation for a few more years, this time in my possession. I had hoped to repair the window and mount it in a hanging frame in our home, but I lacked the skills to accomplish even that task. Forgotten, it lay in the darkness on a shelf in the closet of our guest room. The years passed.

The course of events changed for the window as our church welcomed into our fellowship a woman with extraordinary artistic gifts in various media, one of which was the design and creation of beautiful objects of stained-glass. When she heard of the broken and disintegrating pile of lead and scratched stained-glass in a box in our closet, she eagerly volunteered to undertake its renovation. A few weeks later, a stunning work of beauty was returned to us. Broken antique glass had been replaced with exact replicas. Old, twisted "lead came" was replaced, binding the glass pieces together into one spectacular window, appearing again in its original splendor. We carefully stored it away again in a special box awaiting the day when an oak frame and chain would hold it once again proudly in the light of the sun. The years passed once again as the beautiful stained-glass window lay safely in its padded protective box.

One winter, a series of violent storms flooded our roof, overwhelming the gutter system directly at the front entry of our house. Water leaked through the roof, ceiling and walls, soaking the front door and causing the veneer to buckle and split. The damage was considerable. With our front door damaged and now dysfunctional, we were forced to search for a replacement door.

Specialty doors are very expensive, from a few thousand dollars to many thousands. Our door was wider than a conventional one and slightly shorter. Without the resources to purchase an expensive item, we were faced with making our own custom door. Our long-time friend and elder in the church, Brian, suggested visiting a firm which specialized in architectural items, featuring used doors, windows, hardware and interior decorations. These recycled objects were for sale at a fraction of their normal cost. There we found a door. Although it was scratched and missing some of its veneer at opposite ends; top and bottom, Brian assured us that we could find a functional door in that scratched and chipped item before us. Plunking down $10 for the used item, we lugged it home with hopeful anticipation in our hearts.

While we were away for a few days, Brian, a skilled craftsman in his own right, created a magnificent solid-wood front door from that used, discarded reject which now fit the intended opening of our house perfectly. Best of all, he had placed the stained-glass window into the door. His artistic wife determined the color and finish of the door, laboring with her husband to produce a polished and eye-catching finish. What a surprise when on the first sunshiny day, hues of gold, green and maroon mingled with the warm rays of sunshine flowing through the portions of clear glass, dispelling the darkness from that corner of our living room!

Even more surprising, we later found out from our daughter and son-in-law, missionaries in Germany, that the emblem in the center of the window was the coat of arms for the German province of Baden, where they lived in the quaint village of Kandern and labored for the Lord. Apparently, the window had indeed once beautified a German Pentecostal church in Portland, now long since vanished into the mist of history.

It took years for the once-broken pieces of a beautiful stained-glass window and a discarded, damaged door to come together. But now we gratefully remember the artistic skill of Brian Lohr and his lovely wife, Becky, who contributed their efforts to create our front door from that which was broken and so severely damaged.

And as we exit and enter our house through our beautiful front door, we are reminded again and again of the creative grace of God, who supplies all our need. Something old and broken and useless became a thing of beauty. It reminds us often of the change in broken and useless lives promised in II Corinthians 5:17: "Therefore if any man be in Christ, he is a new creature: old things are passed away; behold, all things are become new."

35

At Just the Right Time
June 2011

The itinerary of our Europe trip was exciting! After a day spent in Kandern, a quaint and picturesque village in the southwest corner of Germany, visiting our daughter and son-in-law and our two teen-aged granddaughters, the plan was for my wife, my well-travelled brother, Charles, and me to spend a few days in Carmona, Spain. From there we proposed to take day trips to some of the incredible Spanish and Moorish art and architecture at several nearby historical sites. As an added opportunity, we hoped to include a day's drive south to the English peninsula of Gibraltar to view that unique community situated on the slopes of the largest monolith in the world. Returning to Germany after four days in Spain, we would attend the high school graduation ceremony of our granddaughter, Kailyn, at the Black Forest Academy in Kandern, which constituted the most important part of our trip.

After a tiring eleven-hour flight from Portland, Oregon to Zurich, Switzerland and a one-and-a-half hour drive from Zurich to our destination, we finally arrived at Kandern, just a few miles from the border between Germany, France and Switzerland. Grateful to be reunited with family again, we rested a day before boarding a plane for the east coast of Spain.

Upon arriving there without incident, we rented a car at the Seville airport and, with Charles at the steering wheel, drove through the pleasant countryside with olive-tree-covered hills and scenic valleys to the small city of Carmona (where the ruins of the palace of Pedro the Cruel still can be seen). Our destination was an old hotel on the southeast side of the city. Situated at one side of an historic town square, it joined other shops facing the square. The ancient architecture of the buildings gave the scene an air of intimate community. Between the shops and the square was a circular, single-lane, one-way road separating the square from the pedestrians, who sauntered along the cobblestone walkway in front of the buildings. The narrow road encircling the flat area of the square was paved with large, hand-cut stones. Beautiful, leafy trees shaded ornate benches, which offered not only a resting place for the aged but also convenient spots for tourists and visitors. The rapid cadence and musical pitch of the Spanish language flowed between young mothers and aged grandmothers, who also were keeping a watchful eye upon the happy children who ran and played in the open space of the community square. In the center of the round paved area (the "square") was a fifteen-foot-tall ornamental wrought-iron pillar set on a large base of polished white marble. At night, eight large light globes affixed to the pillar by curved arms of wrought iron illuminated the area, causing the trees to cast their shadows against buildings surrounding the square. Even though the curved road separated the square and the buildings, it seemed to fit into the artistic charm of the surroundings, adding a sense of space in the confines of the area.

The historic architecture of our hotel was worn by the ravages of time, yet it retained the charm of a former age when life was less hurried. The romance of history was evident in the smallest details of decorated tiles, curled wrought iron fences, rails and gates, and surprisingly beautiful architectural features. In the center of the hotel, a small open courtyard was flanked by tile steps guarded by a wrought iron rail. These led to rooms on the second and third levels. Colorful flowers bloomed from pots of various sizes and shapes set in the nooks and crannies of the roofless atrium. The ambience inside the hotel made us feel that we had stepped back several generations.

It never occurred to us that staying in a hotel several hundred years old might constitute a hazard to our health. The age of our assigned room along with the considerably worn condition of the walls and floor must have made cleaning and maintenance quite difficult for the hotel staff. However, blithely we hung our clothes and distributed our toiletries, unaware of the possibility of virulent germs hiding in the crevices and cracks in the floor. The stained, broken and discolored tiles in the bathroom should have impressed us to be more cautious with our hygiene, but, from wherever they were hiding, the germs attacked us with a violent result. At the end of our second day in Carmona, I felt nauseated with intestinal upset. All the symptoms of digestive illness accompanied my extreme discomfort. Weak and unable to roam far from the bathroom, I was confined to our hotel room in the old historic building which, though heavy on atmosphere, was light on cleanliness and comfort.

Even the cordiality of the management and the warmth of the people at the local restaurants around the square did not offset the complete illness I began to feel. Carolyn and Charles went sightseeing without me on the third day while I stayed in the hotel room with nothing to do but make frequent trips to the bathroom.

On the fourth day, even though Carolyn now began to feel ill, we dressed for the trip to Gibraltar, not wanting to miss this once-in-a-lifetime opportunity. The trip was demanding, and Charles carried all the driving responsibilities. Carolyn and I were of little use in reading maps and pointing the way, even when we got lost in Seville.

In Gibraltar, we drove the narrow streets, looking for the road to the cable car parking lot. The extreme traffic was unimaginable. We spent hours driving around the town of Gibraltar, often stuck in traffic jams but never able to reach the top of the Rock of Gibraltar. Angry, frustrated and defeated, we realized that it was time to return to our hotel in Carmona.

When we left Spain the next day for the return trip to Germany, the layover on the isle of Majorca was more of an ordeal than a pleasure. But I sensed that the worst was over for me. Even though Carolyn was beginning to feel the ravages of illness more acutely, I was beginning to feel my old self again. My sense of relief would have disappeared had I known what lay ahead.

Arriving safely at the comfortable accommodations of our daughter and son-in-law, Carolyn and I were glad for family support and the relative comforts of home. Our relief was short-lived.

The next afternoon, while David and Catherine were away at a school function, I was suddenly struck with spasms of abdominal pain which I had never experienced before. Waves of agony swept over me as I nearly fainted from the severity of the ordeal. For over an hour, I writhed and twisted under the assault of some hidden cause. There was no way to contact David and Catherine. I only knew that I could not endure much longer.

When David and Catherine returned, they rushed me to the local medical office in Kandern. Fortunately, the Doctors Gearinger had established their practice there. A husband and wife medical team, these doctors knew Catherine and David and admitted me immediately to their emergency room. Recognizing some severe physiological problem, they immediately offered me a palliative, called an ambulance and rushed me off to the Helios Clinic in a nearby village, where more complete tests could be analyzed to determine the cause of my agonizing distress.

Later, I learned that David, our son-in-law, had made the decision to send me to the exclusive Helios Clinic in Müllheim rather than the government hospital in Lörach, which was part of the German socialized health care system. The Helios Clinic was a new, upscale facility, only three years old, located on the outskirts of the small hamlet of Müllheim among the hills of the Black Forest. As an American with private insurance, I was given a room in an exclusive wing of the hospital, reserved for those who could afford priority treatment.

It turned out to be a fortuitous choice and exposed me to my first close-up experience with German thoroughness. A team of three doctors met me that evening and immediately administered a battery of diagnostic tests; blood analyses, electrocardiograms, x-rays, ultrasound and a general physical exam. After a conference, the team assigned to my diagnosis determined that I had suffered an acute gall bladder attack. The surgeon in charge of the team gravely informed me that had I delayed a day, I would have died. Therefore, they were scheduling my surgery early on the second morning. They would carefully monitor my condition and spend the next day stabilizing me prior to surgery. Even though I was too ill and in pain at the time to fully appreciate the level of care I was receiving, I was impressed by the clinic's efficiency. In the United States, the tests would have taken a matter of several days, if not weeks.

The language issue was not a large problem. My French nurse was a small, 60-year-old woman who spoke little English but hovered over me as a fussy mother over a sick child. Every bit as competent as the younger German nurses, she compassionately attended to my every need, checking on me frequently throughout the night. The single male nurse, who also worked at night, hailed from Ukraine and spoke passable English. In the late night hours, when I was awake, he would spend time with me in conversation about his own experiences and how he came to be working in a German hospital. Such communications made my lot much easier. How difficult it would have been had I not been able to understand what was transpiring around me. Fortunately, my own former experience as an army surgical specialist prepared me for life in a hospital.

The surgeon, his team and all the surgical specialists spoke fluent English, which allowed them to communicate to me the details of my condition, my diagnosis, my prognosis, and the details of my after-hospital care. Even in my crisis, I was not panicked by the fact that I was alone in a German hospital, with my care entrusted to people whom I did not know, in a culture foreign to my own, away from my network of friends, and about 30 miles away from family. I was alert enough as I lay on the operating table to appreciate the brisk efficiency of the surgical team. I felt that I was in a familiar environment once again even though the hospital in Japan where I had served over 50 years ago did not compare to this modern, state-of-the-art operating room.

My surgery was laparoscopic. Four small inch-long incisions in my abdomen were all it took to insert the necessary instruments to remove the gall bladder, cauterize the blood vessels, and staple the pertinent tubes. Four band aids covered the incisions, which healed in a matter of days. Internal healing took a little longer.

Boredom in the hospital was not an issue until after surgery. The modest television mounted on the wall opposite my hospital bed carried nothing but German programming and a sports channel featuring game after game of football (soccer). Turning the sound down to eliminate the distraction of the excited commentary of the German sports reporters, I soon grew weary of that sport. Other than German TV, all that was left to me was reading the magazines and books that David and Catherine, Charles, and Carolyn brought to my room on their visits. My waking hours were punctuated by many periods of deep sleep.

The hospital room was spacious with large picture windows which offered a panoramic view of the trees of the Black Forest. A single road wound through the landscape up to the hospital. Entertainment consisted of watching for the occasional automobile or emergency ambulance that travelled the road to and from the hospital. When I recovered enough to walk the short distance from my room at the end of the wing to the central lounge area, I could see through other large windows, the beautifully painted cottages across the road, framed against the lush greenery of the forest. It was truly a beautiful, almost "fairy-tale" setting. Beyond the cottages, surrounded by the trees of the Black Forest, a grassy meadow sloped upward to the ridge of the hill.

White clouds floated in a bright blue sky. The picturesque and peaceful scene served to lessen my post-surgical stress.

I was fed a diet of "cremesuppe" (cream soup). The soups were varied (cream of asparagus, cream of rutabaga, cream of broccoli, and cream of cauliflower). While they were tasty (and most likely healthful), the soft diet soon became tiresome. By the time I was ready to leave the medical facility, I had resolved to avoid cream soups for the remainder of my life (a resolution which I quickly abandoned after tasting again the homemade soups of my wife).

The day I was released from the Helios Clinic, the staff came by one at a time to say goodbye to their "American patient" and to wish me a speedy recovery. Apparently, the news that there was an American patient in the clinic had spread throughout the hospital. When I left, I was presented with a very nice zippered kit full of toiletries accompanied by sincere good wishes for my complete recovery and a remainder of a successful vacation.

It had taken only four days from my entrance to Helios Clinic to my release. I went back to Kandern, having recovered sufficiently to eat normal food and to walk around the village, exercising moderately. By the time of Kailyn's graduation, I could move without hesitation, attending her commencement ceremony with some degree of energy and vitality.

While the temptation lingered to bemoan my ill-fortune at having contracted an illness in Spain and a further gall bladder infection in Germany, I could not indulge in such self-pity. The obvious Hand of God had been clearly evident.

1. Had I suffered the attack on the plane part way across the Atlantic Ocean, I might have suffered many hours before reaching adequate medical help. When I told my experience to a flight attendant on the flight home, she opined that the plane would have diverted to the

nearest airport in Greenland, Iceland, Holland or England. In any case, it might have destroyed our plans completely.

2. Had I suffered the attack in Spain, I would have been at the mercy of the Spanish health care system. When I suggested the possibility to my German surgeon, he threw up his hands in horror and cried, "God forbid that you should come under Spanish medical care!" Apparently, the Germans have little regard for the Spanish medical establishment. While I recovered at the Love's home, an epidemic of swine flu broke out in Germany. The Germans immediately blamed the Spanish for the contaminated vegetables which were being exported to Germany, and the German government immediately halted all Spanish imported vegetables pending a thorough investigation. The Spanish government, in return, was livid with indignation and threatened to recall their ambassador in response to the unfounded allegations. The war of words escalated in the newspapers and on German television for a few days during my post-hospitalization recuperation. It finally died down after the culprit was discovered to be vegetables from northern Germany.

3. Had my gall bladder attack occurred a few days later than it did, I would have missed Kailyn's high school graduation.

If there is such a thing as a perfect time for a crisis, this was it. Too much earlier and the trip would have been jeopardized, expenses would have risen and the timing of the schedule damaged. Too much later and I would have missed Kailyn's graduation and possibly the returning flight home. Undoubtedly God's hand was over the entire situation.

Later, after we had returned to our home, our insurance company covered all the expenses of the crisis as if it had occurred in the United States. What a perfection of timing! God did supply all our needs "according to His riches in glory by Christ Jesus."

36

God's Minivan
May 2013

Carolyn has always had the gift of looking ahead, especially where family is concerned. Whenever some insight or awareness flashes into her consciousness, she stores it away in the memory banks of her mind for later retrieval at the opportune time. It was when we were spending a day at the pool of close friends some years ago that a persistent idea lodged itself firmly in her mind. Our hosts had just showed us their recent purchase of a deluxe, late model Honda Odyssey van with all the extras and luxury accessories. It was a technological marvel. Our hosts had acquired it at a bargain price since their daughter was one of the managers at the car dealership.

Viewing the car, Carolyn declared, "We need a van! With our expanded family, we could travel together on vacation trips." "And," she added, "with all the things we haul, we could use the extra space." It made sense. We had often traveled with the members of our family in one vehicle. Now that the family had expanded to include grandchildren, a larger vehicle with extra space could be most useful. "We can't afford a van like this one," I protested. "Besides, we don't need a new expense just about now." It was a useless remark on my part, for Carolyn was always thinking of family. Of course, our friends were delighted that we should aspire to such a remarkably comfortable and roadworthy means of transportation and encouraged us to look for a recently pre-owned van comparable to theirs. Alas! When we investigated online, we discovered the hard truth that such a purchase was far beyond our financial capabilities. We simply could not afford even an aged Honda Odyssey. Any van not more than six years old with relatively high mileage still commanded a price far beyond our modest means. Still, Carolyn did not abandon her dream for a van.

Her dream was reinforced two years later when we travelled to Germany to see our daughter and son-in-law and our granddaughters. They had planned a vacation to Scotland and England in their late model Mitsubishi van with the expectation that we would enjoy the vacation with them. In the relatively spacious confines of their van, we drove through Germany and France to Amsterdam, Holland, where we caught an overnight ferry traversing the North Sea to Newcastle Upon Tyne. From there we drove a leisurely trip to Edinburgh, Scotland, then down through England to London, and on to the east coast. There we loaded the van onto the train that took us underneath the English Channel (in the Chunnel) to France. After this exceptional experience, we drove on to Brussels, Belgium and finally to their home in Germany.

It was a memorable trip, not only because of the fabulous sightseeing and the experience of sampling other cultures but also because of the relative comfort of our travel. Riding in a van rather than in the cramped confines of a sedan made the trip much easier and far less fatiguing.

The merits of a van capable of carrying a load of six or seven passengers, compared to the smaller space inside an automobile, was indisputable. Although she did not mention it, Carolyn's anticipation of van ownership cemented itself into her mind even more permanently. Her vision was that when her family came from Germany to visit, it would be a wonderful convenience to carry us and our visiting family to common destinations. Meanwhile, it would afford us greater space when Mark and Suzanne travelled with us to Yakima to visit Carolyn's sister and brother-in-law.

However, the opportunity to purchase an affordable van did not present itself. But Carolyn never lost her dream. As a few years passed, the "van dream" receded, an unrealistic fantasy. When we lacked the means to transport some of the Howie estate back to Oregon City following the death of Carolyn's father on January 11, 2013, the lack of a van became an even greater disappointment. The estate having been settled, each of the surviving children received items meaningful to them. Carolyn's portion, packed in several boxes, was too large of a load to carry in our automobile. Aside from that, the inheritance included a recliner, a decorative wood chair, and a large, three-unit set of matching furniture which included a hutch, a desk and library shelves. Our ten-year-old Camry lacked even the power to pull a small covered trailer necessary to bring the load from Yakima to Oregon City, a 220-mile distance.

Even though Carolyn carried her grief privately following the death of her second parent, I knew how much a tangible reminder of her parents meant to her and was determined to do whatever was possible to bring those items back to our home. A little over a month following the news of her father's death, I was shutting down my laptop toward midnight. On an impulse, I activated my e-mail program to see if any new messages had arrived.

Only one message appeared which had been posted only a few minutes before. It read: "We are downsizing..." and listed a "2002 Town and Country minivan. $3,995. One owner, 115,000 miles, power steering, air cond., power locks, privacy glass, cruise control, AM/FM CD stereo, dual sliding doors, roof rack, alloy wheels." It was from some close friends of ours. It seemed like a golden opportunity to meet a current need and to fulfill Carolyn's long-held dream for such a vehicle. Although Carolyn had already prepared to retire for the evening, I informed her of the e-mail. Her response was enthusiastic. I sent a return e-mail immediately, setting up an appointment to see the van the very next day. It turned out to be even more than we had hoped for with new tires and a computer package which monitored tire pressure, gas mileage, estimated time of arrival and other exciting features.

It was a used vehicle with only one body defect, a small crease in the hood, where they had struck a deer some time earlier. Upon examining the hood with its thin rust line, I joked with them that for the price of the vehicle, they should have at least thrown in the deer, allowing us to celebrate the purchase with venison steaks. They looked at me blankly until they apparently decided that it was not a reflection of my mental incapacity, but my feeble attempt at humor, upon which they politely laughed. We did not try to bargain with our friends about the price. They had done so much for us, had been so generous, and had placed such a reasonable price on the van that we agreed on the terms without hesitation. Besides, we considered the availability of the van to be a clear work of God on our behalf.

Our son, Mark, sanded the rust spot a few weeks later and applied a coat of primer to the van. The spacious interior of the van allowed adequate room for cargo when the third row of seats was removed. With the trailer hitch which Mark lent us, we rented a small covered trailer and hauled all the necessary possessions from the Howie estate home.

The van served another important purpose shortly after its acquisition. In the summer months of 2013, our granddaughters came to visit us for the summer. Both are licensed drivers. Daneille immediately got a job and drove one of our vehicles to work each day. Kailyn also drove our car while her sister was at work. It became even more important when David and Catherine arrived for six weeks at the end of the summer, for they also had need of transportation. However, Carolyn and I were not left without a vehicle to drive because of our purchase of the van, which became the third vehicle in our driveway. Even with six licensed drivers in the household for those six weeks, we were able to manage the busy schedules of everyone in the house. It was a blessing from the Lord, who knew in advance what our transportation and hauling needs would be in the spring and summer of that year.

The van proved to be a very comfortable and reliable vehicle; one which afforded us joy in driving with a clear capability of hauling larger items as the occasion demanded. A few months later, we contacted the automotive department of our local community college, which repaired and repainted the hood. Once again, the Lord provided for our needs far beyond our imagination.

37

The Piano
April 2014

It seemed strange at first; the enchanting sounds of a piano floating on the warm air of a lazy summer afternoon in 1942. But the rich harmonies of an unseen musician had caught my attention. As an eight-year-old boy intent on finding a playmate with whom to while away the leisurely afternoon hours, I was just a few houses short of my destination when the music fell upon my ears.

The neighborhood on Dominion Avenue where my journey had taken me was neat and attractive, the well-kept houses surrounded by yards bordered with leafy shrubs and colorful flower beds. Tall trees shaded the sidewalk from the summer heat, yet leaving warm sunny spots between the reach of their branches. Only a few houses ahead of my destination, flowing musical chords fell upon my ears. Played by a skillful pianist, the intricate melody emanated from the interior of a nearby neighborhood home. I stopped to listen.

Yes, my parents, brothers and I heard the piano and organ being played every Sunday at the church which our family attended. In fact in my childhood I must have thought that pianos and organs belonged primarily in churches, theaters or civic auditoriums. Even our school auditorium had a piano, though no one ever seemed to play it at assemblies. Yet here in the quiet of a summer afternoon, music was coming from a house just ahead.

Even though I did not recognize the tune, I was entranced by the music and, before pressing on my way, determined that someday in my house as an adult there would be a place for a piano. A musical instrument to bring a new dimension of beauty and artistry into a home and provide a gracious additional sound to life to my simple childish mind, was a social mark of living high above that of our family's existence. Thoughts of cost, age, condition, style or model never crossed my mind. I only remembered the peacefulness that I felt as the gentle and gracious notes permeated my being on that warm summer afternoon.

Permanently etched, that determination lay silently dormant in my mind for the next 26 years.

During those growing years, I graduated from high school, received a college degree, served for two years in the military, and spent four years in seminary. During my seminary years, I courted a beautiful young woman and married her shortly after graduation. Our three children came within the next five years.

In 1967 our young family moved to The Dalles, Oregon to serve in the field of Christian Education at the Calvary Baptist Church. The deacon chairman, Dick Roth, was a large, genial man who owned the local music store, which dealt with musical instruments large and small as well as top-of-the-line electronics. Dick's wife, Dorothy, was the primary musician and choir director in the church. Both vibrant Christians, they generously shared their love and friendship with our growing family. Remembering my childhood experience and sensing an opportunity, one day I approached Dick about the purchase of a used piano. With our meager salary, I could not afford a new instrument. Hoping to purchase an inexpensive piano, I was unprepared for the generosity of the Roths, for one day Dick appeared at our door with an old 1895 Chickering piano firmly belted to a mover's hand truck. Dick deftly maneuvered the piano through the front door and into our living room.

Whatever original gold gilt the piano had once proudly displayed was now gone; only a shadow of the original design was evident. Many of the original ivory keys had disappeared, exposing bare wood where the valuable coverings had once shone so brightly. There was no mistaking the fact that the piano had a sorry appearance. In addition, some of the keys did not depress to produce the sounds of the appropriate note. To determine the cause of the problem, Dick quickly removed the entire keyboard with the extraction of a few screws. To our total surprise, genuine flint arrowheads lay on the panel below the keys, blocking their action and an old coin lay among the arrowheads. Dick surmised that the family from whom the piano had been traded as part of a downpayment on a newer instrument must have had small children who delighted in inserting objects between the keys. However, once the obstacles were removed, the piano played easily, even if somewhat out of tune.

Doubts still lingered. I did not know anything other than that the old instrument was worn. The original finish was gone. Weighing more than 400 pounds, it was difficult to move. Some of the beautiful veneer had cracked. Uncertain that it fit the décor of our house, I did not instantly recognize the beautiful provision of the Lord.

In fact, the old Chickering piano was a classic, quality piano, easily tuned to play with a rich, warm sound that enhanced the various harmonies produced under the artistry of a skilled pianist. But with so many ivories cracked, discolored or missing, the piano was not a pleasure to play. Yet at least we did have a piano. Best of all, Dick and Dorothy had made a gift of the piano to us.

In 1970 our young family found itself in a church in Cottage Grove, Oregon, with no pianist. I had been called as the pastor for a small, struggling congregation. Although the church had purchased a beautiful, new spinet piano, there was no one to play it for the worship services. Thus for many services we simply sang without accompaniment. For many weeks I longed for a pianist whose talents could enhance the quality of our worship services.

One day, early in our ministry there, I read Exodus 31:1-6 as part of my morning devotions. I finished the first six verses of the chapter before a realization dawned upon my mind. I read:

"And the LORD spake unto Moses, saying, See, I have called by name Bezaleel the son of Uri, the son of Hur, of the tribe of Judah: And I have filled him with the spirit of God, in wisdom, and in understanding, and in knowledge, and in all manner of workmanship, to devise cunning works, to work in gold, and in silver, and in brass, and in cutting of stones, to set *them*, and in carving of timber, to work in all manner of workmanship. And I, behold, I have given with him Aholiab, the son of Ahisamach, of the tribe of Dan: and in the hearts of all that are wise hearted I have put wisdom, that they may make all that I have commanded thee." (Exodus 31:1-6)

Stumbling over the unfamiliar names, I realized that God was providing help for Moses so that he could accomplish all that God had required of him in building the ornate tabernacle. God even named his helpers. As I read, I reasoned that *if God could do that for Moses, why could He not do so for us? After all, Carolyn and I were called to help build up the church in Cottage Grove. Surely God could send people to help us in that noble task.* I prayed, asking God to send us someone who could play the piano. But for several weeks nothing happened.

However, before long a family moved into Cottage Grove to work at the local lamination plant and the Howards began to attend our church. Martha's husband was a successful tool designer for large mill equipment. Martha was a gifted pianist and a dedicated believer. Furthermore, she was willing to play the piano for all services.

During that time an obvious truth formulated itself in my mind. I learned that Martha's parents had gone to the expense of providing their daughter with piano lessons. They had sacrificed for their daughter to practice and learn a difficult skill. At her parents' expense and her own expenditure of time and effort, Martha had learned how to play the piano with sufficient skill to accompany a worship service. It was not a mature skill that came suddenly upon her, but one learned and honed by hours of diligent practice. And now our church was benefitting from the sacrifice of her parents, who had paid for piano lessons for their daughter so many years ago.

In discussing the issue, Carolyn and I decided that we were obligated to pay back this benefit by investing in piano lessons for our three children. Perhaps one of them might develop enough skill to enrich the worship of some other church. Fortunately our two girls pursued piano lessons with interest. Our son's interests lay elsewhere. His heart was clearly not in the musical arts. We did not recognize this until years later, when he naturally excelled in the computer sciences and made them his life's vocation.

After a period of two years, Martha and her husband moved away from our community, his work calling them to another mill town far away. Again we were without a pianist for church services.

However, by this time our two daughters had taken enough interest in piano to learn some basic skills. Little did Carolyn and I anticipate that the church our daughters would be helping was our very own congregation. At first their accompaniment was primitive, yet it helped the congregational singing. The church members were very gracious with their appreciation for these two fledgling pianists, and before long the two girls were playing for services with some improved skill.

As our daughters went on to college away from home, the Lord provided an outstanding concert pianist for our church. In an act of gracious generosity upon the occasion of the death of my mother, this talented young wife and mother replaced all the ivories on our home piano keys during our absence at the funeral services in California. The piano was now a delight to play with its shining keys, warm tones, and rich timbre. Piano music filled our home when our daughters returned from college and played the old instrument with a proficiency we had not yet witnessed.

By the time we moved to a church in Oregon City, both of our now grown girls were highly skilled musicians, playing regularly for church services. They became proficient in accompanying congregational singing, soloists, and musical groups as well as playing special musical presentations themselves. Because they enjoyed playing our piano, they arranged that whenever the church pianos were tuned, the tuner would come to our home as well to perform his tuning skills.

Sometimes, when I returned home after a weary day of ministry, my spirits would be buoyed by the beautiful sounds of music coming from our home. Even the neighbors expressed their appreciation at the harmonious sounds wafting over the neighborhood.

The circle was now complete. Not only had God provided our family with a piano, but He had steadily provided pianists to help us in the completion of the work God had called us to do in building up His church.

Who would have thought that a boyhood determination so many years ago would become an adult reality by the grace of God?

38

In Retrospect

My parents were devout believers who were active members of the Immanuel Baptist Church in Pasadena, California. While my chronically ill mother missed attending many services because of her illness, the rest of the family attended services every Sunday and prayer meeting every Wednesday evening. I virtually grew up in church. My father conducted family devotions regularly in our childhood years. But it was not until I was eight years old that I accepted Jesus as my Lord and Savior in a Child Evangelism class in our neighborhood, to the delight of my parents.

With my new spiritual awareness, I grew slowly in the Lord. Because our church was in near-proximity to many Bible schools and seminaries, it was not unusual to hear a noted evangelist, Bible teacher, seminary professor or missionary as a guest speaker. It was a common occurrence to hear illustrations and stories, many from personal experience, of the near-miraculous works of the Lord. While listening to stories of divine activity in the affairs of mortal beings, I did not view that as everyday experiences of the average believer. Unfortunately, the impression which I received was that those nearly miraculous stories happened to someone else, not to me. The thought became embedded in my mind that those wonderful works of the Lord were reserved for men and women of unusual spirituality. They were beyond my limited Christian faith. Yet, even with my lack of faith, the Lord called me into the ministry.

As I grew into young manhood, I attended a Christian liberal arts college and seminary. It was then that I began to realize that God could provide for my needs in dramatic ways. I began to realize that those stories I had heard in my home church during my growing years were not exceptional, not reserved for "super-Christians," but marvelous evidences that God is active in the lives of even the humblest believer. The reasoning grew within me that the same unseen God of the Old and New Testaments, who performed marvelous works on behalf of His followers, even those who doubted Him, was the same God in whom I trusted.

We do not have to be giants of the faith for the Lord to work on our behalf in wonderful ways. We simply need to trust in His promises. The Bible is true when it says: "But my God shall supply all your need according to his riches in glory by Christ Jesus." (Philippians 4:19)

Printed in the United States
By Bookmasters